Dancing Naked
Under Palm Trees

To order additional copies, please contact us.
BookSurge, LLC
www.booksurge.com
1-866-308-6235
orders@booksurge.com

EVELYN
CRAWFORD ROSSER

DANCING
NAKED UNDER
PALM TREES

2005

Dancing Naked
Under Palm Trees

DANCING NAKED

No Images

She does not know
Her beauty,
She thinks her brown body
Has no glory.

If she could dance
Naked,
Under palm trees
And see her image in the river
She would know.

But there are no palm trees
On the street,
And dishwater gives back no images.

Waring Cuney

To Dorothy Everson, My Friend Whose Belief In Me Inspired Me To Write This Book.

CHAPTER 1
MY OWN WORST ENEMY—1952

I had fun today. My best friends, Shirlie and Alice, came by to play with me. Mama told us to play outside. She had a cake in the oven and didn't want it to fall. We played a game of make-believe. Shirlie was Elaine Stewart. Alice was Jane Russell. I was Marilyn Monroe! I lived in a beautiful house on the beach. Every evening I took my French poodle for a long walk. I loved to feel the sea breezes on my face and the surf gently lap against my feet.

Shirlie made me mad. She said I am chocolate, and everybody knows only white ladies have poodles and live on beaches. She said she could live on the beach because she looks like Lena Horne. I started to cry. That's when Alice made Shirlie shut up. Alice said it didn't matter what color I was when I was born. I could bleach my skin. She knew it for a fact. Her cousin Betty did it. She used something called Black and White Ointment. She rubbed it on her face and neck every morning and night. Alice said the only problem was I couldn't let the sun strike me. Her cousin Betty never went outside without a hat or scarf on, 'cause if you do you'll turn blacker than you were before. I trembled at the idea. I'll miss playing with Shirlie and Alice, but I want to live in a fine house someday like the white ladies do.

I'll ask God to speed up my bleaching.

***

We spent the night sitting in Mama and Daddy's bedroom around the heater chewing cane and telling stories. Daddy's were the best. I enjoyed his stories, but he made me scared to go to bed. I think I'll sleep with the cover over my head tonight. I hope I don't dream about the headless woman walking down the railroad track or the horse that wouldn't move unless the rider gave him a drink of moonshine. Sometimes I think Daddy makes these stories up.

He ended the night by telling about the end-of-the-year program in Douglas, Georgia. Daddy lived out in the country on a farm called Huffas. To get her teaching contract renewed at the end of the school term, the teacher had to have her students entertain the superintendent and the board of all-white members. Daddy said he was in a skit about slavery.

He loved to tell this part. Daddy got up from his chair and acted out the rest of the story for us. He said he wore a straw hat and overalls with one shoulder strap hanging down. He was barefooted. All the students were lined up in rows of fives, holding rusty hoes in their hands. The guests sat quietly staring in anticipation. The teacher waved to the pianist to start the music. Daddy said the students started moving slowly, pretending to chop cotton.

They sang slowly and mournfully:
"Ma's told me
Ma's told me
To stay on
De old plantation."
"Ma's told me
Ma's told me
To stay on
De old plantation
Where de cotton do grow."

Daddy said at this point in the skit, each student took a handkerchief from his back pocket and wiped his face. The song continued:

"Lord um tired
Lord um tired
Of dis heavy
Load I keep a-totin'
Totin', totin'."

Then he said they began to chop wildly and move fast down the imaginary rows of cotton, singing:

"Oh, a nigger sho kno'
How to make things gro'
By marchin' down de rows
And choppin' wid a hoe."

The guests started yelling, "Ye ha! Well done, Miss Caroline. Best program ever!"

Daddy said Miss Caroline's face beamed with satisfaction. She knew she had her job for another year. The fire left Daddy's eyes as quickly as it had appeared. He looked sad. He mumbled something about it being wrong for her to use them like that. Daddy said, "Negroes shouldn't use other Negroes to get what they want." I didn't know what he meant, but I knew something bad had happened to Daddy. Almost in a whisper he told us to go to bed. It hurt me to see Daddy sad. I'll sleep with the quilt over my head tonight. That way no one will hear me cry.

***

I became the neighborhood hero today. I was so proud of myself. I finally did it! I went into old Mrs. Pearson's yard. Everybody says she's a witch. She never goes anywhere during the day, but I heard she rides a broom at midnight. She lives a block from East Parkway Elementary School, so the only way to get to school is to pass by her house. Every day on the way home from school, we always do something to upset her. Most of the time we throw rocks at her porch. "Run before the old hag gets you," someone always warns. Usually we run while screaming our heads off. The same warning was given today, but this time everyone ran except me. I was going to show them that Mrs. Pearson didn't scare me.

All of us children have always been told that if we touched the marigolds in her yard we would turn into a snake. Mama had told me that if was scientifically impossible for that to happen, so I decided to touch the flowers. I ran into her yard, touched the petals and ran like crazy. Just as I was leaving, Mrs. Pearson opened the door and yelled, "You ugly little girl! Get out of my yard before I turn you into a snake." At the sound of her voice, all the children started running and screaming. I ran until I was out of breath. When I thought I was safe, I stopped to rest. Everyone crowded around me patting my back. I tried not to show it, but I could feel my body trembling in fear.

Mama asked me why I was so quiet during supper. I couldn't tell her. She would have whipped me for bothering old Mrs. Pearson. Instead, I told her I had a headache. The truth was I was scared that at any moment I would turn into a snake and slither all over the dining room table. That would have been the end of me. Mama's terrified of snakes, and she would've killed me for sure. From now on I'm going to be good so I can live to be as old as METHUSELAH.

***

We went to Douglas, Georgia to visit Aunt Carolyn yesterday. She's Daddy's oldest sister. She and Uncle Rick don't have any children. She says they've always wanted children, but God never gave them any. Grandmama says that God is too wise to make a mistake. I know I wouldn't want Aunt Carolyn to be my mother. She's too mean. I'm scared from the moment we walk into her house until we leave for home. She walks around with her lips poked out, grumbling about one thing or another. She is either complaining about being sick or about Uncle Rick doing something she didn't want him to do. I don't think I've ever seen her happy.

The truth is, I really don't care to visit her. There's nothing for Noah, Gabriel, and me to do. There are no games or toys for us to play with. Mama tells us to stay inside, so we sit at attention like soldiers waiting to hear "Dinner is served." Actually, we're never excited about eating dinner. Aunt Carolyn is a lousy cook! I've never been able to figure out why it takes her three or four hours to fix dinner when all she does is open up some canned food and make cornbread. Yuck! Her cornbread is the pits. It's flat and as hard as a brick. Aunt Carolyn says it's "real" cornbread. She brags that she makes it for the communion at church. I wouldn't want it, but it seems to fit the purpose. Jesus wants Christians to be humble, and if anything can humble a person, it's Aunt Carolyn's cornbread! Do we ever tell her how we feel about it? No, we sit and eat, and then lie about how much we enjoyed our dinner. She swallows the lie, and we're booked for another visit.

You would think we'd had enough, but we had another visit to make before we could return home. As usual, we waited until it was dark before going across town to visit one of Aunt Carolyn's friends. She lives in the projects. She has beautiful blonde hair, but her teeth are scattered around in her mouth. Her mouth looks dirty. I don't know if it's her rotten teeth or the snuff she dips. I don't mind the hard squeeze she always gives me when we first arrive, but I hate when she kisses me good-bye. One time I wiped her kiss off my face, and Mama chewed me out all the way home. Now I just let her squeeze me and tell me how I look just like my daddy. To keep peace with Mama and Daddy I let her salivate all over me.

The ride home seems to take forever. I can't wait to wash my face.

***

I loved the doll I got for Christmas. Daddy broke it today. You see, it was an accident. My brothers took the doll from me and were throwing it back and forth over my head to one another. When I ran to Noah, he threw it to Gabriel. I told Daddy to make them give it back to me. He came into the bedroom and told them to stop throwing my doll. They didn't. He got angry. He snatched it from Noah and threw it to me. I didn't catch it. The doll hit the trunk. Its head was broken off. I cried. Daddy promised to buy me another doll. Mama told me to stop crying, because a nine year-old girl was too old for dolls anyway. She said dolls only make girls want babies. She doesn't know me. I don't want a baby. I want a mink coat, red convertible, and a big house on the beach.

Tomorrow I'll have a funeral for my doll, and I won't invite Mama.

CHAPTER 2
THANKFUL FOR MY PARENTS—1953

"Train up a child in the way he should go and when he is old
he will not depart from it."

Proverbs 22.6

***

Ralph, Charles, and Leon tried to rape a lady today. They attacked her in the woods behind East Parkway Elementary School, but she beat them and marched them to the principal's office. She didn't want them to go to jail, so the principal, Mr. Bailey, called their parents. The parents agreed for the principal to whip them in front of their classmates. Leon's daddy said he'd rather see him whipped at school now, than to have the police do it later in jail. He was convinced Leon was following the wrong crowd and headed down the wrong road.

All of us students sat quietly. I felt sorry for the boys. The principal put a chair in front of Mama's desk (she was our substitute teacher). He asked the boys which one of them wanted to get his punishment first. Leon volunteered. Mr. Bailey told him to lie across the chair and to begin reciting the Lord's Prayer. Then he struck Leon as hard as he could.

Leon said. "Our Father, which art in heaven."

"Go on. Continue!" shouted Mr. Bailey.

Crying, Leon looked up at him and said, "I don't know no mo!"

The class snickered. Mama rolled her eyes at us. The room was silent again. We didn't want any part of the principal's strap.

Ralph and Charles never received a lick because when Mr. Bailey asked them if they knew the Lord's prayer, they too shook their heads indicating no. Their punishments were to learn the Lord's prayer.

I feel so sad now about laughing at Ralph, Charles, and Leon. It seems like I've known the Lord's prayer since the day I was born. My parents have us to kneel beside our beds and say a prayer each night. We even have to say a Bible verse before each meal. I'm so thankful for my parents. I'll tell them how much I appreciate them tomorrow.

***

I'm having fun with my new brother Matthew. He's only four months old, but he already knows me. He really does! I enjoy walking him to sleep every night, but I still don't understand why Mama and Daddy had another baby. They're too old! Mama's thirty-two and Daddy's every bit thirty-four. It's really embarrassing. I don't understand how she got pregnant anyway. Mama told me she and Daddy don't even kiss, so how in the world did they make a baby?

I dreamed Mama was going to have a baby. I was scared, but I mustered up enough nerve to tell her about my dream. When I told her I dreamed she was going to have a baby, she told me I'd better be careful myself. I told her I didn't have anything to worry about, because I've never even seen a naked man before. To my surprise she laughed. Mama doesn't like to talk about sex, so I took her laugh to mean that she was going to have a baby.

When it came time for Matthew to be born, Daddy gave us some money and sent us to the movies. He didn't ask us if we wanted to go; he just ordered us out of the house. Noah was responsible for our safety to and from the movies. When we reached Lee Street, Noah announced, "Daddy sent us off so Mama could have a baby."

"The doctor's not there," I said.

"Why does she need a doctor?" Gabriel asked.

"To cut out the baby," I replied.

Gabriel blurted out, "The doctor don't cut your stomach open to get the baby out."

"Then how does it get out?" I asked.

"Mama grunts and strains the baby out," Noah volunteered.

"I'm going to tell on you for talking nasty," I warned.

"You'll see I'm telling the truth when you have your first baby," he said.

"I'm never going to have children," I announced.

We continued on in silence. I didn't want to hear any more talk about grunts and groans. Besides, I didn't want Noah and Gabriel to know that I knew very little about having babies. Girls are supposed to know about things like that. It was only when I was reading a True Romance that I learned where babies come from. Grandmama always told me that the midwife brings them in her little black satchel. I wondered how they got enough air to stay alive and imagined that she punched holes in the bag. I never asked because I didn't want to sound childish.

I tried to enjoy the movie, but I couldn't stop thinking about Mama. I couldn't imagine any part of her body large enough for a baby to come out of. Maybe grownups' bodies were different. I just didn't know.

Somehow it must not have been as bad as I had imagined. When we got home, Mama was sitting up in bed smiling, proudly displaying a new baby named Matthew.

I love him with all my heart.

***

Daddy got awful mad with me tonight. It was all Gabriel's fault, but no one would believe me, not even Daddy. Somebody had been stealing Daddy's cigarettes for months. He kept warning us that he would beat the living daylights out of the person he caught smoking his Camels.

Today I caught Gabriel smoking in the back yard. When I first found him I told him I was going to tell Daddy. He begged me not to tell and then told me to just take a couple of puffs on the cigarette. I did. Then he said, "If you still want to tell on me go ahead, I won't be mad. But before you do let's play a game."

"What kind of game?" I asked.

"It's called good-luck," he explained. "You're the high priestess. You bring good luck to everyone. In order to bless someone you must march around the cigarette butts seven times and say 'woodchuck, good luck'."

I did as Gabriel said, repeating, "Woodchuck, good luck," while he did an Indian chant.

"Oh, you're really bringing us good luck now," he said. "But to be sure we have good luck march around seven more times."

I marched around the butts, counting as I went.

"Awesome!" Gabriel said. "Your footprints will bring us good luck."

I wanted to play longer, but he told me he had to go to the outhouse.

I was in my room reading when I heard Daddy calling Mama.

"Come here, Candy. I found our smoker."

I went to the kitchen to look out the window and couldn't believe my eyes! There were puffs of smoke coming from the outhouse. I almost fainted. I knew if Daddy had caught Gabriel I was in trouble too. I had cigarette smoke on my breath!

Daddy sneaked up to the outhouse and snatched open the door, shouting triumphantly, "I've caught you. You're the one who's been stealing my cigarettes."

He marched Gabriel into the kitchen.

"No," my brother protested. "I caught Baby Girl smoking these cigarettes and she gave them to me!"

I was stunned." You're lying," I shouted, taking a swing at him.

"Come here," he said. "I'll show you."

He led Daddy to the corner of the house where we had played the good-luck game and pointed to my footprints.

"This is where I caught her smoking."

Daddy turned to me and ordered me to blow, so I closed my eyes and blew breath into his face.

"I'm going to whip you when the baby wakes up," he said. "Why'd you do it?"

"Gabriel told me to," I answered.

"Yeah! You're going to get a good licking."

"Are you going to whip Gabriel too?"

"No," Daddy answered. "I have something better for Gabriel."

He took Gabriel to the house and handed him a fresh pack of cigarettes. I thought Daddy had lost his mind. Then he did something that made me *know* he was crazy. He told my brother to eat them. Gabriel was trying to act tough. He cocked his head to one side and placed a Camel in the corner of his mouth. He sucked it in, chewed, and swallowed.

"Not bad," he said. "I think I'll have another one."

Daddy was not amused. Mama, Noah, and I sat quietly watching. By the time Gabriel got to his fifth cigarette, I could tell he was getting sick. His eyes watered, he gagged and started throwing his guts up..

"I guess you've had enough cigarettes to last a lifetime," Daddy said.

Then he turned to me. "You will get yours when the baby wakes up."

I went to my room and prayed for the baby to die. I figured if that happened, Daddy and Mama would be too upset to think about whipping me. But Matthew didn't die, and I didn't get a whipping. All Daddy did was talk to me, but his talk hurt me worse than any whipping I've ever gotten. I could look in his face and see that I had disappointed him. He explained to me that I had let him down, not because I had tried smoking cigarettes, but because I had let Gabriel think for me.

He sat on the side of my bed and told me a story about a man who built two boats. Daddy said the man designed his boat, purchased the materials and began building his boat. He knew exactly the kind of boat he wanted.

A man came along and asked, "What are you doing?"

"I'm building a boat," answered the man.

"Well, you're doing it wrong," the stranger said. "Let me show you what to do."

The man watched carefully and began to imitate the stranger. The stranger strolled off happy that he had helped someone.

Another man came along and asked the boat builder," What in the world are you doing?"

"I'm building a boat," he answered.

"I hate to tell you this, buddy, but you're doing it all wrong. Let me show you how to do it."

Again the builder watched his new teacher demonstrate the proper technique for building a boat. When he felt secure enough to build the boat the way the new stranger had showed him, he took the hammer from the man and began working furiously. As time passed, different people came by and gave him suggestions on how to build his boat. He used each person's suggestion.

Finally, the boat was finished. The man believed the boat was seaworthy. After all, he had received advice from so many people. He took the boat out to sea, and it sank! When the man recovered emotionally from the loss of his first boat, he decided to build another boat. Just like the first time, he designed it, purchased the materials and began building.

"What do you think happened?" Daddy asked.

"I don't know," I said.

A stranger came alone and asked, "What are you doing?"

"I'm building a boat," answered the man.

"If I were you I wouldn't do it that way," offered the stranger. "Let me show you what I'd do."

"No thank you," said the boat builder. "Do you see that pile of junk over there?" the man asked pointing to a heaping of wood and iron.

"Yes," answered the stranger.

"Well, that's everybody's boat." Patting the side of the new boat, he said, "This is going to be *my* boat. I'm building this one all by myself."

Later the builder took his boat out to the ocean. It sailed across the deep blue sea.

"What does a story about a man building a boat have to do with Gabriel and me smoking cigarettes?" I asked.

"What I'm trying to tell you, Baby Girl, is build your own boats. Whenever you do something, right or wrong, do it because you want to do it, not because someone else told you to do it.

My arms found their way around Daddy's neck all by themselves. He knew I understood.

***

Grandmama, Cousin Ruth, and Daddy killed two hogs today. Mama sort of stood around and watched. Daddy and Grandmama grew up in the country, so they know all about killing hogs and taking out their insides. Grandmama said you always kill hogs on a cold day. I stayed in the house because it was too cold for me!

Mr. Davis came over to help Daddy cut up the hogs. Daddy gave him some meat as payment. Mr. Davis kept telling Daddy he sure could use a little something to heat him up. That was his way of asking for a drink. Mr. Davis and Daddy started disappearing off and on into the woodhouse. That's where Daddy keeps his corn liquor. Some time later, Mr. Davis said he was sick. Daddy told him to go on home. He and Grandmama would finish the hogs. Mr. Davis stumbled down the road toward his house. For his sake, I was glad he lived only two blocks away.

Mama, Grandmama, and Daddy stayed outdoors most of the day making lard and soap. When it got dark outside, they moved everything into the house. I'm glad they did, because Grandmama showed me how to make sausage. I enjoyed stuffing the casings. We made two kinds—one with red peppers and one without. Grandmama put some ground meat aside to make sausage patties. She said she likes to change up sometimes, but it really didn't matter to me. I don't eat sausage, but I love to do things with my grandmama.

***

Mrs. Baylor has been absent from school for two weeks. She is having those headaches again. She thinks there's a tumor in her head. She said sometimes her head feels like it's going to burst open. She said she's often prayed that it would, because she would welcome anything that would stop the pain—even death.

Mama surprised me today. She let me walk with Alice and Shirlie to visit Mrs. Baylor. She was surprised to see us. We couldn't stay long, but we had enough time to tell her what everyone was gossiping about at school. She was hurt when she learned that Ralph, Leon, and Charles had tried to rape a lady, but she wasn't surprised. They were always in some kind of devilment at school. We could tell she wasn't feeling well, but she laughed when we told her about the mother who came to school to kill Mr. Bailey. Someone told him a lady was looking for him. While he hid in the clinic, his secretary told the parent he wasn't at school. The lady cursed and yelled out threats for a while, but she calmed down after she couldn't find Mr. Bailey. When he came out of hiding, he was trembling. Sweat popped out on his forehead when he learned the lady had been swinging a butcher knife around. We never did find out what she was so angry about.

The most tragic incident that had happened while Mrs. Baylor was absent hadn't happened at school. It had happened on a Saturday night at my friend's house. Her mother had gone to prepare dinner for her sick mother. Pebo and Saul, Rosa's two brothers, weren't home and her father came home drunk. Finding Rosa Mae alone, he had raped her. When her mother came home the next day, Rosa Mae told her what had happened. Her mother called the police. Her father was arrested, but he returned home a couple of days later. The news spread like wildfire, and the kids started teasing Rosa. For a while she was in a fight almost every day. Then Ralph, Leon, and Charles had tried to rape that lady in the woods behind the school, and the attention had shifted to them.

I heard the grownups talking about Rosa's rape, and they said her Mama shouldn't have put her father in jail if she hadn't intended to keep him there. Mama said all she had accomplished was embarrassing her daughter. Mama's friend said if it had been her daughter she wouldn't have needed the police. She would have waited until the next time he got drunk to get her revenge. While he was passed out cold, and he usually was, she would have tied him to the bed, heated a bucket of grease, and poured it all over his body.

Mrs. Baylor didn't like that idea. She said we must not respond to evil acts with evil. She said God will punish the wicked. She said we can't let bad people influence us to be bad. She told us to always remember the words of Booker T. Washington: "Don't let no man drag you so low until you hate him." She told us to forget what we had heard, because we had received ungodly counsel.

We seemed to have upset her, so we told her we had to leave. We really did because we had to be home before sundown. She made us promise to come back to see her. I promised, but I didn't want to. I knew I had no power to keep my promise. It was up to Mama.

Dear God, I pray that Mrs. Baylor gets well. I love her so much.

***

We had a chapel program for our class. Mrs. Seaborn wants to teach the importance of eating vegetables in our diets. She says everyone should eat vegetables daily in order to be healthy. She asked us to volunteer for the parts we wanted. Everybody wanted to be broccoli, spinach, cauliflower, tomatoes, and carrots, but no one wanted to be a cabbage. After trying unsuccessfully to persuade someone to be a cabbage, I raised my hand and said I would be a cabbage. The class snickered. I didn't understand what was so funny. I don't like the way cabbage tastes, but Mama loves it. You just steam it lightly and pour a little bacon drippings on it. The trick is not to overcook it. Cabbage doesn't taste good if it's too mushy. I know, because I overcooked mine the first time, but I got it right the next time.

I actually liked being a cabbage today. Daddy plants cabbages in the garden, and they don't look like other vegetables. They're different, and I like being different. Mama says being different takes courage. Anybody can be a copycat any day of the week. It takes no imagination and no brains. That's what Mama says. But to be different, now that's another story. Mama says I should be a pioneer. Do what no one has ever done. Dream dreams no one else has ever dreamed. Be brave! Be different! I didn't really want to be a cabbage, but I did it because I knew that's what Mama would have wanted me to do.

Do cabbages grow in California?

***

Sometimes I don't understand myself. I know I'm smart. Everybody else says I'm smart, but I can't learn to tell time. Everybody else in the class can, and I don't want them to know I can't. They would tease me. Even dumb old Patrick who can't read can tell time. What is wrong with me? I'm getting pretty good at fooling people, though. Mrs. Seaborn thinks I know how to tell time because she always sends me to look at the clock in the principal's office. I just ask Mrs. Moore what time it is. She gives me a funny look, but she always tells me the time, and then I go tell Mrs. Seaborn. It would be so simple if I could just tell time. I guess it's like learning to tie your shoes. I had a hard time, but I finally learned. I'll just have to keep on trying.

***

We had fun at school today. Mrs. Seaborn brought in a cardboard post office. It had a window where we could buy things just like the one downtown. Mrs. Seaborn was the cashier. Before she opened the post office, she showed us how to fill out money orders. We had to find out how much change she owed us. I pretended I was ordering a $15.98 sweater from Belles Hess. She charged me fifty cents for the money order. We had to find out how much change she owed us. I gave her a play twenty-dollar bill. She gave me three dollars back. I told her she owed me fifty-two cents more. She told me that was excellent because she was cheating me. She tricked some people, but she didn't trick me. I can't tell time, but I can count money! Besides, when I go to the real post office with Mama, she lets me pay for the money orders and stamps. She says I need to know how to do these things in case of an emergency. She says I should always depend on myself.

***

I got a whipping today. Crazy Eddie told a lie on me. Mrs. Carter went to town. She told crazy Eddie to write down the names of all the students who were talking while she was

gone. Whose name was first on the list? Mine! The last time
Mrs. Carter went out of the room I took names. I told on crazy
Eddie because he was talking. He put my name on the list to
get revenge. Everyone in the room knew I hadn't said a word,
but no one would tell Mrs. Carter I wasn't talking. She always
tells us, "The good has to suffer with the bad." She said if
anyone talked, the whole class would be punished. She kept
her word. She gave everyone in the class three licks with the
ruler. The licks didn't hurt, but I cried anyway. I was angry. I
hadn't done anything wrong. Mrs. Carter needs to change her
rules. They're stupid!

***

I don't like recess; the teacher makes me go outside. I'd
rather stay inside and study. I would love to play on the merry-
go-round and sliding boards with Alice and Shirlie. I can play
patty-cake, hop scotch and other non physical games, but
Mama told me not to play games where there was a chance I'd
get hurt. I take books outside to read, but Mrs. Seaborn makes
me return them to the classroom. She says recess is fun time,
but I can't get her to understand that I don't have fun watching
other people play. She says I need to relax my brain, and I tell
her it's not tired; I enjoy learning.

Today I decided to play. I targeted the sliding board.
After all, Mama would never know as long as I didn't get hurt.
It looked so easy. All I had to do was walk up the steps, sit
down, and slide. Nothing could be simpler. I got in line and
waited my turn to mount the steps. I was scared of falling,
but I climbed up anyway. I carefully tucked my dress in on
both sides and began to slide. The take-off was exciting, but
halfway down the slide my mouth flew open in a panic. I felt
like an idiot! How could I forget it had rained this morning?

The slide, old and rusty, would ruin my dress. I tried to stop halfway down, but my speed pushed me on. I knew I was in big trouble, but I tried not to look worried. I knew Mama was going to kill me.

Time flew by. It was one o'clock. Time to go home. Time to face mama. My dress was ruined. The front was clean, but the back was rust-stained. I walked home at a slower pace than usual. Each step was filled with dread. Mama's face broke into an infectious smile when she saw me. I returned her smile with a nervous one. When I reached the porch, I rushed to show Mama I had made A's in all my classes. I knew that would please her. I was trying to keep her busy, so she wouldn't see my dirty dress. The telephone rang. Mama told me to go inside and answer the phone. That's when I knew I was really in trouble. I quickly backed into the living room. The call had been a wrong number. As soon as I came back on the porch Mama said two words: "Turn around." I obeyed.

That's when she started in on me. I stood silently and listened to the same speech I had heard a thousand times. I didn't try to explain what had happened, because nothing I said would have made any difference. If she had told me once, she had told me a thousand times: "Cleanliness is next to Godliness". Cleanliness was next to nothing! I had always tried to keep my clothes clean, but I always managed to waste ketchup, mustard, or soda on them. My clumsiness always messed up Mama's plan. I was to wear one dress Monday and Tuesday, another dress on Wednesday and Thursday, and another one on Friday. I wanted to wear a different dress every day and repeat the dresses the next week. It didn't take a genius to see that it was the same difference, but I couldn't explain that to Mama. She would accuse me of sassing her. The penalty for sassing was a backhand slap. The thing that most amazed me was she could always make contact between her hand and my face without looking back. It was like she had a built-in antenna.

I expected to get one of those slaps today, but I didn't. I stood still, looking downward. I really wanted her to think I was sorry for ruining my dress. When she finished scolding me she said, "Tell me how you got the rust on your dress." I did. She looked at me with an expressionless face. Then she said, "Tell me one more time!" I did. To my surprise, she just walked away. I was nervous all throughout dinner, expecting her to talk about it at the dinner table, but it never happened. Instead, she told daddy that I had made all A's today. I knew she was just making polite conversation, because I always made straight A's. It just comes naturally. I'm the smartest one in my class. Now all I need to do is learn how to keep my clothes clean. When Daddy asked who wanted to bless the food, I volunteered. Not only did I bless the food, but I also threw in a few extras like "Bless my wonderful, understanding mother."

***

Today my brothers and I went to the movies. Last week Dick Tracy was trapped in a well. I had to know whether he got out alive. On the way to the movies, we noticed a new ice cream parlor. My brother Noah said we each had enough money to buy a five-cent cone. Gabriel wanted strawberry. Noah wanted vanilla. I wanted chocolate.

A teenage white girl was standing behind the counter. When we approached her, she walked away and busied herself cleaning a table. We stood at the counter and waited for her to finish cleaning the table. We waited and waited. She turned her head to look at us and started wiping the table again. By that time my brother Noah was mad. He knocked hard on the counter several times. The girl didn't turn around. Noah knocked again, this time harder. The girl ran from the room. A mean looking man came out, drying his hands on a stained apron.

"What do you want?" He yelled at us.

"We want some ice cream," Noah answered.

The man just stared at him.

"I mean, we want to *buy* some ice cream," my brother added. The man continued to stare.

Then he said, "We don't serve niggers here!" He walked away leaving us alone at the counter.

My brother Noah wanted to jump across the counter and smash his face in. I begged him not to. I didn't want Noah to get into trouble. I could do without the ice cream. We went to the movies, but I had a hard time keeping my mind on Dick Tracy. Today was the first time someone had ever called me a nigger to my face. Mama was right. I'm getting too old to play with dolls. There are more important things to think about.

***

Today I did something that I'm ashamed of. I was caught stealing Grandmama's chocolate drops. Grandmama was so disappointed with me. I would have felt better if she had hit me, but she didn't. She just got an awful, suffering look on her face and said, "Uh-uh-uh." She said it over and over again as she shook her head in disgust. I felt so bad for hurting my grandmama. She has always taught me to be honest and trustworthy. I have tried so hard to do right, but I have one weakness. I love chocolate—chocolate cake, chocolate candy—anything chocolate!

Whenever Grandmama discovered we children had done something wrong, she would sit down and talk to us. If we admitted we were wrong, she would be all right. It was another matter if we denied any wrong doings. She would say, "Just keep on doing what you're doing. I'm going to give you enough rope to hang yourself." That's what she did today.

Grandmama has a trunk that we children can never go into without her permission. One day she sent me into her trunk to get a shawl for her. While I was looking for the shawl, I saw a box of chocolate drops. I asked her to give me a piece, but she told me to wait until she had opened the box. Several days later I peeped into her trunk and saw that the candy box was open. I ate just one piece. Days later, I ate another piece. This continued for weeks. Today I decided to eat another piece, but when I reached into the box, it was empty. I had eaten all of Grandmama's candy!

I eased the trunk lid down and headed for the door.

"Did you find what you were looking for?" Grandmama asked from behind the door.

I was too surprised to say anything.

"Why didn't you just ask me for it?" She continued, "I'd rather give you the candy than to have you steal from me."

"I wasn't stealing, Grandmama," I protested.

"Did you have permission?" She asked.

"No ma'am," I said as I looked everywhere except at Grandmama.

"Then you stole the candy," she insisted and walked away shaking her head. "Uh-uh-uh."

She hadn't said very much, but at the same time, she had said everything she had needed to say. I fell across the bed and cried myself to sleep. When I woke up, a Baby Ruth candy bar was lying next to me. I began to cry again. Grandmama was love in action. She had always told me to hate the sin, but love the sinner. I had stolen her candy, but she had still loved me. Sometimes I think I love my Grandmama more than I love anyone else in the whole wide world.

Mama took me window-shopping to help me get over feeling bad about taking Grandmama's candy. I cherish the time we spend together. Most of the time Mama is off working, cleaning house, cooking, or trying to teach us kids how to behave properly. I accuse her of fussing at me all the time, but I know she only wants me to become the finest person I can possibly be. She's told me a million times, "Baby, all I want is the best for you."

Most of the time she's so serious, but when we are alone she tells me stories about the family. At these moments I feel so close to her, and I want to be just like her. She's so beautiful. Her figure is shaped like a Coca-Cola bottle. I'm as thin as a pencil, and sometimes my brothers call me Olive Oyl. I hope my chest fills out like Mama's. She assures me that I will blossom in time.

Today she told me a story about a man named Vernon who was cheating on his wife. She said years ago the kitchen was made off from the main house. The married man's girlfriend was a cook for a rich white family. When Vernon went to see his girlfriend he always met her out in the kitchen. They never turned on the lights, because no one was supposed to be in the kitchen at night. They didn't want to attract any attention. As fate would have it, Gertrude (the regular maid) had a massive heart attack, so a new maid was hired immediately. The new maid just happened to look out the window and saw Vernon coming out the kitchen door. He had been planning his date with the cook. The maid didn't want Vernon to see her, because she was a dear friend of his wife.

When Vernon left, the cook came inside to get some clean dinner napkins. The maid hadn't finished ironing, so she asked the cook to sit down, and they could get acquainted while she finished. In reality, she had wanted the cook to open up to her and tell about her relationship with Vernon. As she suspected, the cook spilled her guts, and the maid received more information than she had expected. The cook had told her how turned off Vernon became at the sight of his wife's naked body. There was no desire left. He only stayed with his wife for the children's sake. Not only did she tell her the most intimate details about their affair, but she also told her when Vernon would be by to "fulfill her desires" as she had modestly stated with a grin.

The maid hung on to her every word, but she tried not to appear overly interested. From time to time she said to the cook, "You shouldn't be telling me this," but she did nothing to quiet her. She wanted all the facts to relay to her dear friend. She especially found it hard to contain herself as the maid told her that Vernon's wife did not like "to be bothered". She had raised her eyebrows to show her own pleasure. She knew it was true, because he had told her. He had called his wife "frigid" and kissed the cook's feet as he told her how much he appreciated a passionate woman. She thought he was the most romantic man in the world.

The maid had wanted to defend her friend and protest, "No, that's not the way it was. Vernon came home drunk every night. When he wasn't drunk, he found something to start a fight about." But her hands were tied. If she had said anything, she would have exposed her hand. So she bit her tongue and suffered as the cook disparaged her friend. But sometimes justice is swift. The maid told Vernon's wife about his date with the cook. As fate would have it, the cook's mother became deathly ill, and the cook had to leave suddenly. She hoped if she wasn't in the kitchen he would have enough sense to go home. She convinced herself that she couldn't worry anymore about it. She had to go look after her mother. She had no other choice. She knew Vernon loved her. He had told her that as many times as there are stars in the sky. She had nothing to worry about. He would save his loving for her and *only* her.

Filled in on the details, Vernon's wife stuffed her corset with rags to give herself a plumper figure. Even though she had planned to have no physical contact with him, there was the possibility that he might touch her. If he had insisted, she would have had to mumble, "It's my time of the month." She had everything planned to the smallest detail—even to the drops of perfume her friend had given her to put in her knee bends.

As soon as dusk disappeared, she had crept into the kitchen and waited for Vernon. She had hoped the thumping in her chest wouldn't give her away. Her loud breathing was also an annoyance. Nevertheless, she waited and waited. She was about to give up and go home when she heard him whistling. When they had first married, he had whistled all the time. Later the whistling gave way to grunts, sighs, and hissing through the gap between his two front teeth, signs that announced his boredom and disappointment. She had tried to erase her ideas, but she realized that she wanted to hear him whistle that way while he was coming home to her. Jealousy flooded her body. She stood motionless in the dark. He would have to make the first move. To her amazement, he did not come completely inside. He peeped his head in just enough to give her a message.

"Mariah," he whispered as his eyes searched the dark room.

So now she knew her competitor's name.

"Are you here, Baby?" He asked, more tenderly than she could remember him speaking to her in ages.

"Uh huh," she grunted. Anything more and he might recognize her voice.

"I know you're going to be disappointed, but I can't stay tonight."

He walked to the colonial table in the middle of the room without even feeling his way. She knew he had walked that path many times before. He turned in the direction of the silhouette reflected in the moonlight.

"I brought you a ham," he said. "The next time we're together I want you to cook me some ham and eggs. We'll have a good ole' country breakfast."

He moved closer to the shadow and said, "I know I haven't had a bath, but I can't leave without touching you."

He reached over, grabbed both her shoulders, and kissed her brazenly. The kiss told her that he wanted more, but she just stood still with her arms hanging limply at her sides.

"I got to go," he said hastily.

"All right," she answered, just loud enough for him to understand her.

He was gone, and she stood in the dark and cried momentarily. Then she took the short cut through the woods. That way she could beat him home, get into bed, and pretend to be asleep. Her swift feet delivered her home first, and she had lain awake all night waiting for dawn. At five-thirty she had breakfast ready. When Vernon went into the kitchen, his eyes almost bulged out of his head! A platter of ham and eggs was at his seating place. At first he was suspicious, but soon dismissed it as a coincidence. He ate heartily. When breakfast was over, he picked up his lunch bucket and went into the fields as usual.

Even though the ham and eggs had not been prepared by his beloved Mariah, he had still enjoyed his breakfast. He wondered what Elvira would have for dinner. She seemed to be in a cheerful mood, and he wondered what had brought that about. Women were like the weather—unpredictable. Nevertheless, he looked forward to going home to dinner, but when he opened the door, the smell of ham slapped him in the face. He couldn't believe his eyes! There was another plate of ham and eggs at his seating place.

Vernon wondered what Elvira's motives were, but he dared not ask her about the ham and eggs. He couldn't ask Mariah, because she had not returned to work. So he ate the ham and eggs until the sight of the food made him sick to his stomach. For five days Elvira had served him ham and eggs. During his waking hours, all he thought about was ham and eggs. When he closed his eyes at night he dreamed about ham and eggs. He could even be heard mumbling to himself, "Damn ham and eggs, damn ham and eggs."

On the seventh day, Vernon snapped. He hurled his plate across the room as he screamed," Why the hell do you cook damn ham and eggs everyday, every meal?"

"Don't you remember?" Elvira asked sarcastically. "You told me to cook it for you."

"I didn't tell you a damn thing," he shouted back.

His wife was adamant. "Oh, yes you did! Don't you remember the night in the kitchen? Let me refresh your memory. The line that keeps echoing in my mind is 'I know I haven't had a bath, but I can't leave without touching you'."

Vernon raised his hand to slap her, but the surprise was too much. The left side of his face began to quiver, and the left side of his body became numb. He had had a stroke. Out of pity, Elvira stayed with Vernon. He recovered a year later. He became her "go for". She said she could get him to do almost anything for her, but she could never get him to eat ham and eggs!

Mama burst into laughter. I laughed, too. I didn't find

the story as funny as she did, but it was wonderful to see her laughing.

**

We didn't sleep at all last night. We were terrified that the Ku Klux Klan would burn down our house or drag us out and lynch us. Mama threatened to kill a white man yesterday. It wasn't her fault, but that wouldn't have mattered. All Negroes know it's not healthy to stand up to a white person, but Mama did it.

Yesterday Mama was sitting on the porch plaiting my hair when a white salesman parked in front of our house. I was sitting on the floor between her legs facing the road. The salesman called Mama to his car to look at the merchandise he had for sale. He said he had all sorts of pretty clocks, pictures, cloth, dishes, and chenille spreads. Mama told him she had all the household items she needed. Unwilling to give up, he told Mama he also sold pianos. For a small down payment, he would have the piano delivered. He told Mama he had a catalog she could look through. She asked to see the catalog. She didn't want the piano for herself; she wanted it for me. She knew I fantasized about becoming a celebrated concert pianist and needed to practice daily. I had started taking lessons from Mrs. Seaborn, my fourth grade teacher, at her house after school. She said she couldn't deny I had talent, but I couldn't be successful unless I had somewhere to practice. I had learned the keyboard by practicing on a cardboard piano keyboard. I would finger notes and hum the tune as I practiced my finger exercises.

The salesman went to his car and got the piano catalog. The pianos were so beautiful! The sight of them took my breath away. I couldn't wait to own one. I selected the one I wanted. When Mama saw the price of the pianos, she told the salesman we couldn't afford one. Disappointed, we returned to the porch where Mama continued plaiting my hair. The salesman didn't want to lose a sale, so he followed us back to the porch trying to persuade Mama to accept an easy payment plan. He told Mama he had a convenient payment plan that many women liked.

He looked at me and said, "Why don't you send your daughter off to play? Then we can work out the terms of the down payment."

"What do you mean?" Mama asked.

He grinned mischievously at her, winked, and said, "You know what I mean. Send your daughter off for an hour or two."

That's when Mama tapped me on my right shoulder twice with the comb. That was the signal for me to go to the kitchen and get a butcher knife (We didn't own a pistol). Without saying a word, I went inside the house to get the knife. When I returned the salesman was still standing on the porch teasing Mama. I hid the knife behind my back. When I sat down, I laid the knife on the floor under the side of my dress. Mama casually reached down to feel where the knife was.

"Please leave my porch," she calmly told the salesman.

His face flushed red. "What did you say to me, girl?" he asked in an intimidating voice as he looked at Mama with contempt in his eyes.

"You heard what I said," Mama answered without showing any sign of fear..

"Don't you talk back to me," he said. "Can't no nigger sass me like that."

"I just did," Mama said.

To show him she wasn't afraid of him she did the unexpected. She stared straight into his eyes. She knew that white folks liked for Negroes to look down when they talked to them. She knew if anything could rile him, looking him straight in the eyes would do it.

"Girl," he said. "I've got a mind to...." He stopped in the middle of his sentence and raised his right hand to slap Mama. Before his hand could reach Mama's face, she sprung from her seat and placed the butcher knife to his throat. His hand froze in mid air. He backed slowly off the porch. Not once did he take his eyes off Mama. When he reached the safety of the road, he yelled racial threats at us.

"You'll be sorry," he promised. "Nigger woman, you've just signed your own death warrant. I'm going to have the whole lot of you swinging from the highest tree!"

Showing no fear, Mama ran down the steps toward his car. He sped away throwing gravel in every direction. Mama and I rushed inside and locked all the doors and windows. We sat on the sofa cuddled in each other's arms, waiting for Daddy or my brothers to come home. I had never seen Mama shake the way she was. The last time I had seen her this frightened was when lightening had struck our house. It had taken her a long time to get over the incident. Every time there was a thunderstorm Mama would turn off the electrical power and make us sit silently until, as she put it, God had finished doing his work.

I sat in the living room with Mama and wondered about my life. If God could make the lightening flash and the thunder still roll, why didn't He change white people's hearts? Why couldn't He make them understand that we have feelings just like everybody else? We bleed, we love, and we hurt just like everybody else. I'm not asking for much—just to be treated with respect and accepted as a human being. What I want most is to have the opportunity to develop my God-given talents, to have my uniqueness appreciated, and to move to beautiful California.

***

Mama and I went window-shopping tonight. Although she didn't mention the death threats we got yesterday, I could tell she was still thinking about the incident. I also knew she was trying to help me calm my nerves. She knew that looking at pretty things would transport me into fantasyland. As we walked along the dirt road, Mama did most of the talking.

"Did I ever tell you about the time Mr. Jackson sent a worker to take our heater on the coldest day in the year?"

"No, ma'am," I answered.

"Well", he did," Mama continued.

Without waiting for me to say anything, Mama told her story:

"I couldn't believe that man actually sent someone to take our heater. Your brother Gabriel was only three weeks old when your daddy got laid off from the lumber mill. George went to Mr. Jackson and told him he was shooting badly at the moment, but as soon as he got back to work he was going to catch up his bill. Mr. Jackson said he would wait, but I guess he got tired of waiting. George had gotten up around five in the morning and made a fire in the heater so the house would be warm when we got up. Around nine o'clock someone knocked on the door. I couldn't imagine who could be coming to our house that early in the morning. I called your grandmama into the room and told her to see who was at the door. When she returned she said, 'There's two men at the door. They said Mr. Jackson sent them to take your heater. You're $3.00 dollars behind on your payment." I went to the door and told them I had just had a baby, and the heater was the only source of heat we had. The colored man, Jake, said he was sorry, but he had to obey orders if he wanted to keep his job. That's when I got angry. We were only two weeks behind on our payment. I told him, "If you want the heater, come and get it."

Jake and the other worker rushed toward the bedroom. As they opened the door, I could see your grandmama putting more wood onto the roaring fire.

"There's the heater," I announced." "Take it."

Jake looked at his companion. "There's a roaring fire in it. Give me some water to put the fire out."

"'I'm not giving you anything', I said. "'Mr. Jackson told you to take the heater. Now, do what you came here to do. Take the heater to him!'"

"'How do you expect me to take down a stove with a fire in it?" he asked hoping for understanding.

"I don't know and I don't care," I answered.

"You must be crazy," Jake's companion added. "Mr. Jackson can come and get this heater himself.

After they left the house, we laughed hysterically. Mr. Jackson never did come for the heater. Two weeks later your daddy was called back to work. We paid Mr. Jackson off and closed out the account. He said the whole incident had just been a misunderstanding. We had missed payments before, but he had never wanted to take the heater until we were down to our last two payments.

You know, God doesn't love ugly. I don't know what happened, but shortly after that Mr. Jackson went out of business.

Look! Mama exclaimed. The Clothes Box is having a sale tomorrow."

Thoughts of that cold, bitter night soon gave way to

daydreaming about owning fur coats, brass beds, and diamond rings.

***

I love my Grandmama! She is so good to me. I went to visit Miss Lawson with Mama. When I came home, there was a pretty, blue sundress. It was the dress I had showed her in a <u>Montgomery Ward</u> catalog yesterday. She hadn't said a word, but she had given me a big hug. I should have known she was up to something. She told me to go outside and play and not to come back into the house unless it was a matter of life and death.

At six o'clock Mama called out, "Supper." Those words were music to my ears. I don't enjoy ants and centipedes. (I learned in biology class they are not sandy peas). I'm terrified of snakes. They roam freely in south Georgia in our yard, under the house, and in the thicket behind our house. Being outside is cruel and inhumane punishment, but it had been worth it.

I guess Grandmama didn't finish the dress yesterday, because Mama suddenly decided she needed to get Miss Lawson to can some tomatoes for her to make succotash. Daddy grew okra, tomatoes, and butter beans in our garden. Mama hates to can. Grandmama put up fifty-four jars of vegetables before she announced she had put up all the food she was going to can. Mama then started giving food to the neighbors. Cousin Ruth suggested that Mama teach me how to can. I emphatically said, "Give the food to our neighbors." It wasn't that I was concerned about feeding the hungry. I just didn't want to do any work.

I admit I'm a little lazy and don't deserve all the love I receive. I guess I'm just lucky. Everybody in this family goes out of their way to get me what I want. I'll wear my new dress with pride and dignity. It's worth a million dollars to me, not because it's new, beautiful, or costly, but because my grandmama made it for me. I will always treasure it. I love my mama, too. She went out of her way to help Grandmama surprise me.

Both of my mamas are special people.

***

We went to Daytona Beach, Florida to visit my Aunt Judy. In some ways it was fun. In some ways it was not. The fun part was being with Uncle Jimmy. He's Mama's brother and my favorite uncle. Last night, the house smelled like a restaurant. Mama fried chicken, lots of chicken. Uncle Jimmy likes cold chicken. He's from Detroit. He says by the time the food gets to the North it's lost its flavor, so he makes up for lost time when he comes to the South. Mama made a dishpan full of potato salad too. That's my favorite. I like it hot. Daddy bought a cooler and filled it with sodas and placed the potato salad and bologna sandwiches on top. Mama said anything with mayonnaise on it had to be kept cool if we didn't want to die of food poisoning. We ate as we rode along, appreciating the beautiful sights.

I enjoyed the trip, but the car was too crowded. Uncle Jimmy never rides the bus, because he said he was whipped once for not giving up his seat to a white woman. He said he was already in the "colored section", but the white section became filled. The bus driver told him to move to the rear of the bus. Not asked—told! Uncle Jimmy said he didn't move. The driver stopped the bus. The white men beat him and threw him off the bus. Uncle Jimmy laughs whenever he tells the story, because he says he realizes now that he's lucky to be alive. That was thirty-four years ago when he was eighteen and living in the South, but he had never forgotten the incident. Things still hadn't changed much in the South.

The thing that made the trip not fun was we had to hold our water until we saw a station that had a "colored" sign on the bathroom door. Sometimes we would drive for hours before we would find a gas station with a bathroom for colored people. Other times we had to go behind a tree or in the bushes. In Florida, good peeing places are hard to find. (Oops! Mama told me to always say "urinating". That's what educated people say). The land is flat, and the trees are few and far between, to use one of Grandmama's phrases. Uncle Jimmy started getting frustrated, so he said he wasn't going to buy any more gas from anyone who wouldn't let us use the bathroom. He said his strategy would be to never let the gas gauge register below half-full. That way we had choices. Uncle Jimmy said a person should always keep himself where he's never at anybody's mercy. That way you won't have to trade your dignity for survival. It made sense to me.

When we came to the next exit Uncle Jimmy pulled into a gas station in Ocala and told the attendant to fill up the tank. Uncle Jimmy asked the man if he could clean his own windshield while the car was being filled up. The attendant told him he would be glad to clean the windshield for him. He seemed friendly enough, so Uncle Jimmy asked him if there was a restroom. He answered that he didn't have one for colored people, but since we were the only customers present, we could go on and use the restroom. Before he could finish getting the words out of his mouth, a car drove up to the other pump. The attendant looked at Uncle Jimmy with a pleading look in his eyes, and Uncle Jimmy understood. He didn't go to the restroom. Instead, he went inside and bought some Mary Jane candy. When he came back out of the store, the car had driven away.

"I'm sorry, but those were local customers," the attendant

said. "If they saw a colored man coming from my restroom, they would never buy gas from me again."

Uncle Jimmy didn't say a word. He just drove away from the station very fast.

We didn't stop again until we reached Aunt Judy's house.

***

Daddy is a mild-mannered person, but Noah can get his dandruff up. Boy, did he do a good job today! Noah told Daddy that he had never had enough to eat in his life. Now, it's all right to tell Daddy that you've never had a new bicycle. You can even tell him that you've never had name brand clothes, but you should never tell Daddy you've never had enough to eat. That's what Noah was stupid enough to do today. Daddy doesn't care much for spending money on clothes or furniture, but when it comes to feeding his family, he cuts no corners. So when Noah announced he had never been full in his whole life, Daddy said he smelled his own blood boiling.

Veins popped out on Daddy's forehead as he worked silently. He went into the chicken yard and killed three chickens. Mama fried chicken, baked Mexican cornbread, steamed rice and green beans. She sliced tomatoes and made syrup bread. Daddy made two pitchers of tea.

Mama and Daddy put all the food on the dining room table, but there was only one place setting. I thought that was strange. I also was surprised to see *all* that food on the table for lunch. We usually ate hamburgers, hotdogs, watermelon, or cantaloupe for lunch. I decided that today must have been a special occasion I had forgot about, but when I sat down at the table, Daddy immediately told me to get up. The entire meal had been cooked for Noah! He said Noah would never be able to tell anyone else again that he had never had enough to eat and be telling the truth.

Daddy called Noah in and said, "Whenever someone asks you what happened on July 10, 1953, you're going to say: That's the day Daddy gave me enough food to eat'."

Laughing, Noah sat down and said, "Bring on the food. I'm ready." He patted his stomach in jest.

At first Noah gobbled the food down and playfully tapped the side of his glass with his spoon, demanding more tea. Daddy gracefully poured it. The whole time Noah was eating, Daddy stood at the table smiling at him. When all the platters of food had been emptied, Noah pushed his chair back from the table and said, "Boy am I full."

Daddy pushed him back into his seat and said, "No, you're not. Candy, bring out some more food. We want to be sure this boy has enough to eat. We can't have people thinking we don't feed our children. No sir, we can't have that."

Mama took the empty platters into the kitchen and returned with them piled with food.

Daddy said, "Go on and eat, Noah. I want you to have enough to eat."

"Daddy," Noah pleaded. "I was just talking. I never meant what I said. I've had enough to eat."

"No, you haven't," Daddy said. "Now shut up and eat!"

Daddy sat at the table until Noah had eaten everything on the table. Noah cried as he forced himself to swallow, and Daddy continuously filled his glass with tea. When Noah could hold no more, he collapsed on the table.

Daddy got behind him, put his arms under Noah's arms, and clasped them across Noah's chest. He squeezed his arms tightly. That's when Noah threw up in his plate. Daddy really got mad. He screamed at Noah to leave the table. Noah went outside and stayed for a long time. I could hear him gagging.

When Noah came back into the house, he went straight to the bedroom to lie down. Gabriel and I urged him to get up, because we wanted to go to the movies. After begging Noah a hundred times to get up, he reluctantly agreed to go to the movies. He seemed to have been all right on the way to the movies, but as soon as he settled into his seat he began to groan.

"O-o-oh," he groaned, no louder than a whisper.

The next "O-o-oh" was louder. Then he began to groan and squirm uncontrollably. The upstairs usher came over and asked Noah to be quiet. Between moans Noah tried to tell the usher he was sick, but the usher couldn't understand what Noah was saying, so he leaned over to hear what Noah was saying. Without warning, Noah puked all over him.

The usher screamed as he pushed Noah,"Nigger, get out of here."

Gabriel got mad and hit the usher. The usher swung back, but he hit another man. The manager and other white workers joined in the ruckus. By this time everyone in the balcony was fighting. In the midst of the confusion, we slipped out of the theater.

We didn't ask permission to go the movies for a couple of weeks, because we were afraid the usher would recognize us. After all, Gabriel had been put out of the movies once before. He used to go to the restroom, urinate in a soda pop bottle, and pour the urine on the white people downstairs. He said he was letting them know he didn't appreciate having to sit in the balcony, even if the fare was only ten cents. So, Gabriel would have had a time if he had been identified.

Life soon returned to normal. We started going to the movies again, but Noah never again told Daddy that he had never had enough to eat.

***

Noah went to bed feeling very proud of himself tonight. He got even with Daddy for making him eat all that food the last time we had gone to the movies. We were on our own for the movies. We decided not to take our usual route. Instead, we took a short cut through Dasher Lane.

When Daddy left the house, he told Mama that he was going to lay some tile for a man on Hudson Street (Daddy always does jobs to make extra money). I guess that's why I didn't recognize his bicycle parked next to a porch. Noah spotted it.

"Look," Noah said. "That's Daddy's bicycle."

"No it's not," I said, realizing that it did resemble Daddy's bike a little too much for comfort..

"It is too!" Gabriel shouted as he pointed at the bike. "See, there's the dent I put in the fender when I ran into the tree in our yard."

"It sure is," Noah said. "He told Mama he was going to Mr. John's house. He lied!" Before Noah finished his sentence, he grabbed the bike and took off running.

"What are you doing?" I asked.

"I'm stealing his bike," he answered.

We took the bike to the movies with us. When we got home Daddy still wasn't there, and we had seen a double feature. Mama was spitting nails! When Noah told her where we had found the bike, she went crazy. It didn't take me long to realize that she didn't feel too kindly toward the lady who lived in that house! I didn't want to be in Daddy's shoes tonight.

Daddy came in around ten o'clock. To my surprise, Mama didn't let in on him. She even sat quietly as he unloaded on her how someone had stolen his bicycle while he was working at Mr. John's house. I expected Mama to let him know that she knew he was lying. Instead, she told Daddy how awful it was that someone had stolen his bike. When Daddy had snowed Mama (at least he thought he had) he left the room to take a hot bath, which he loves to do all hours of the night.

"Noah!" I heard Mama call.

Noah came.

"Did you do a good job of hiding that bike in the bushes?"

"Yes, Mama," replied Noah. "He'd have to know where it is in order to find it."

"Good," Mama said triumphantly. "I think I'll let him walk to work for two weeks!"

They both snickered.

***

Noah, Gabriel, and I became the proud owners of our first bicycle. Daddy gave us his old one. Then he left the house. When he returned several hours later, he was driving a maroon and gray Studebaker. Mama had been wanting a car for a long time!

Mama can't drive so Daddy drove us around town. We begged him to drive past our classmates' houses so we could wave at them. We wanted everyone to see us in our new car. Actually, it was used, but it was new to us.

"The salesman gave me a good deal," Daddy said. "The owner had been an eighty year-old widower who only went to town once a week."

Mama said, "George, don't be so stupid. The salesman told you that to get you to buy the car.

"No," insisted Daddy. "It's in mint condition. Listen to the engine purr. Feel that cushion ride," continued Daddy.

Before Daddy could answer, the car picked up speed as we rolled down a hill. Daddy mashed on the brakes, but the car didn't slow down. Then he began to pump furiously as he headed straight for the rear end of the car in front of us.

***

Daddy's new Studebaker has brought about many changes in our lives. Mama told Daddy if he could afford a car, he could afford an indoor toilet. She could often be heard saying, "I'm tired of exposing my butt to the freezing weather!" But Daddy's defense was he hadn't had time to build a bathroom. Before we received city water, a pump in the backyard had supplied our needs.

After continued, gentle persuasion, Daddy built a bathroom on the back porch. He hired a licensed plumber to install the pipes when the plumber wasn't working his regular job. That way the job didn't cost as much. Well, when the plumber left, Daddy showed us how to flush the toilet. It seemed like a simple procedure to me, but Daddy kept repeating the flushing. If you ask me, I think he enjoyed seeing the water swirl in the bottom of the commode. I would never admit it publicly, but it fascinated me. I wondered where the waste went. The swirling water reminded me of a tornado I had seen once. Then Daddy gave us the Golden Rule: Always use bathroom tissue. That was all right with me. I had used enough newspaper to last a lifetime.

Having an indoor toilet made me have mixed emotions. It's a little hard to explain, but a part of me was sad. I was losing one of my major means of making money. Whenever the relatives came, especially the older ones, they always hired me to take out the night pots—we called them slop jars. I would have to find another way to make money.

The biggest part of me was happy. I hated squatting over a hole in the outhouse. I had been scared to sit down ever since

Mama killed a rattlesnake in the toilet. It had come inside from the underside. It was so long it covered the entire floor. When I saw the snake, I stuck my foot out to force the door open, but my legs were too short to reach it. That's when I panicked. I screamed loud enough to wake up the dead. Mama came running. She opened the door. Mama stopped dead in her tracks when she saw the rattlesnake. She didn't know what to do. She had never killed a rattlesnake before. She told me not to move. She went to look for something to kill the snake with. She returned with a brick in each hand! The snake hissed and struck out at the air. Mama waited for the right moment to attack it. She smashed his head with one brick and then with the other. Its tail swished wildly. She hurried away and brought back more bricks and piled them on top of the snake.

She reached in and took my hand. I trembled as I walked over the bricks to the door. When I reached the outside Mama hugged me so hard until I thought she was going to crack my ribs.

***

Mama announced to the family that this Christmas would be extra special. Was it possible that I was finally getting my piano? Boy, was I ever disappointed! The big news was that Aunt Judy was coming to spend Christmas with us. She's my favorite aunt, but if I could choose between getting a piano for Christmas and seeing Aunt Judy, I'd choose my piano any day.

Aunt Judy arrived in a long, black car that looked like a hearse. Mama said it was a Hudson Super 6. After Aunt Judy rested a couple of hours she, Grandmama, Mama, and Cousin Ruth went Christmas shopping. While they were gone, Noah suggested we clean the house. He said that way we would get more presents. He could always make up a bed as good as Mama could. She always wondered how he managed to get the bed so smooth. The secret was that Noah beat the cotton lumps with the broom. While Noah made the beds, I washed the dishes. Gabriel stood by ready to mop the kitchen.

When we finished our chores, Noah gave us our promised reward. He unlocked the chifferobe—he knew where Mama kept the key—and showed us our toys. Bags of apples, oranges, and tangerines perfumed the chest. Noah carefully slipped a knife into the opening of a cloth bag and cut oranges into slices with surgeon-like precision. He carefully removed the slices and wiped up any juice that would betray him.

After we had enjoyed the oranges, Noah removed all the chairs from the dining room table. Then he danced into the dining room flashing a mischievous grin. He proudly handed each of us a pair of skates that Mama had hidden in the chifferobe. We skated our hearts out. We took turns being the lookout man. Noah announced that we had better put our skates up before Mama and Aunt Judy came home. Half-heartedly we boxed our skates up, and Noah put them back exactly where he had found them.

Mama and Aunt Judy came home later loaded down with gifts. Aunt Judy raved about how wonderful the house looked. We knew we had done a good job, but we also knew she was just trying to make us feel good. She made remarks about out being sweet, wonderful children that any parents would be pleased to have. I wanted to stop her and confess that we were not wonderful children. We were spoiled, mischievous, and deceitful.

Noah must have read my mind because he gave me a look that told me to keep my mouth shut! To escape his stare, I went to my bedroom and searched the dictionary for a new word to add to my vocabulary. I selected the word salpingectomy.

CHAPTER 3
LETTING GO OF FANTASIES—1954

Everybody has been gossiping about Reverend Byron's Emancipation Day program speech. He was quoted in The Daily Times as saying "For thirty years, I have been telling my people to wait on God, because He still directs the destiny of nations of the world and no man can destroy Him."

He urged, "Do away with segregation slowly." He further declared, "The Southern white man understands the Southern Negro and nobody between Heaven and earth can stop them from loving each other."

Reverend Byron deserves to be criticized. He knows we attend schools without air-conditioning. He knows we get hand-me-down books from the white schools. This year we were told we were getting new books. We did, but the books already had five names in them. Mama said the white kids got the new books, and we got their cast-offs. Reverend Byron knows that Blacks can't stay in hotels or eat in restaurants unless they eat in the kitchen. They can't even *work* in a restaurant unless they're cooks or busboys.

***

Mama received a long letter from Aunt Judy today. She reported to Mama that she is two months pregnant. According to the letter, when she returned home from visiting us at Christmas she became very ill. Everything got on her nerves, and she had trouble keeping food down. She was convinced that she had eaten too much turkey, but Uncle Steve made her go to the doctor. To her amazement, she learned that she is pregnant. Uncle Steve was excited. He has children, but he doesn't have any by Aunt Judy. Mama says this will be Aunt Judy's first baby. She claims to have been pregnant before and had a miscarriage, but nobody in the family can remember the incident.

I'm glad Aunt Judy lives in Florida. That way she won't be able to ask me to baby-sit. If she did ask I wouldn't say no, because I wouldn't want to hurt her feelings. Nevertheless, I can't see myself nursing a baby or changing diapers.

When I get grown, I'm going to have a salpingectomy.

***

Mrs. Q. died today. Actually, she was killed accidentally. Her husband is a mechanic. She loved to tinker with cars. Her car wouldn't start so she pulled up the hood and tried to start it. I don't know all the details or the technical terms to describe what happened, but when the motor cranked, the car took off by itself. It plowed into her house, crushing her to death. I pretended to be sad, but I wasn't. I didn't like her. She was the only person who made me feel ugly and unwanted since the ice cream parlor owner called me a nigger.

Mrs. Q. broke my heart when I was eight years old. Alice, Shirlie, and I were playing outside during lunch. She beckoned for us to come to her. When we reached her, she looked at me and said, "Not you, just these two."

She took Alice and Shirlie into her classroom. She was giving a birthday party for a student in her class. I peeped inside the window. Alice was standing beside her, licking a cone of ice cream. Shirlie was sitting on her lap, kicking her legs happily and also enjoying a cone. Mrs. Q was playing with Shirlie's hair.

I decided Mrs. Q must have thought that I was a nigger too and couldn't enjoy ice cream.

***

I played "That what dreams are made of" over and over tonight. I hope I don't wear it out. I'm so happy. I was kissed by a boy for the first time! There's a dark hall in our school. When the lights go out it's pitch black. Well, the lights went out today. It was only for a few minutes, but Timothy kissed me. We closed our eyes and pressed our lips together. I must admit I was a little disappointed. My toes didn't curl nor did I hear any bells the way the ladies do in the <u>True Confession</u> magazines. I must not be doing something right, but I'm going to keep practicing every chance I get.

I want to hear bells and see stars!

***

Last night we were all gathered around the television set watching "The Ed Sullivan Show" when Grandmama pulled the curtain aside and looked out the window. Peeping out the window every ten or fifteen minutes was a habit of hers. Mama said she was exercising a lifelong habit. Usually when Grandmama looked out the window she peered into nothingness, but this Sunday night was different.

"Oh my God"! She said, covering her mouth with her hand and backing away from the window.

Everybody forgot about "The Ed Sullivan Show" and turned their attention to Grandmama.

"What's the matter?" Mama asked.

At first Grandmama didn't say a word. She slowly raised her left hand and pointed toward the window.

"Look outside," she whispered, "on the school campus."
"Wait!" she continued. "Turn the lights out. They could still be there."

"Who could still be out there?" Mama asked as she headed for the light switch.

Daddy rushed to the window and pulled the curtain back. We could see three crosses burning. Daddy ran into the bedroom. When he emerged, he was carrying his rifle.

"Put that away, George!" Mama shouted. "You know it's the Klan."

"They can't come into our neighborhood and do anything they want to," Daddy said.

"Yes they can," Grandmama said. "They're white folks and we're Negroes. All you're going to do is get yourself killed and this whole family along with you, and for what? Stupidity!"

Daddy calmed down a bit.

"Besides," Grandmama continued. "We don't even know what they want."

We children sat quietly. We had been taught to speak only when spoken to, and this was no time to get on our parents' nerves.

Mama said, "I think I know what's wrong. You remember that Brown girl in Topeka, Kansas was trying to get in that all-white school. It was on the news last week that the Supreme Court voted to end racial discrimination in the schools. Everywhere is going to integrate, including here."

"I think you're right," Daddy agreed.

That was the beginning of a lecture on civil rights that lasted until dawn. Mama told us that white folks were trying to scare us so we wouldn't go to their schools. She said they had been getting away with murder giving us their discarded textbooks while they got new ones. She said the black teachers in Landers County were even paid less money than the white teachers.

When I finally went to bed that night, I couldn't sleep. I didn't want to sleep. I wanted to read everything I could get my hands on. I can't wait to learn. Mama says education means freedom. She says we have to have an education in order to succeed in the white man's world.

I guess the most important thing Mama said last night was I may not always be treated with respect or even as a human being, but if I get an education nobody can take that away from me!

***

Daddy made Mama's dreams come true today. He bought her something she's wanted for a long time—an electric stove! It's one of those RCA Whirlpool's that we saw on television last night.

Mama bought a duck today. That's Daddy's favorite meat. Mama doesn't like it, but she cooks it for Daddy. Mama loves Daddy so much. I want a man just like Daddy. He's the best man in the whole wide world.

I usually go into my bedroom and read while Mama cooks dinner. Noah and Gabriel usually go outside and play baseball. Not today! We sat in the kitchen and watched mama cook. We watched that duck go around and around on the rotisserie. Daddy enjoyed explaining to us how it worked. I could tell he was pleased just saying the word "rotisserie" by the way he emphasized it.

After a while Mama finally said, "That's enough, George. I think everybody got the picture."

I think Mama was a little jealous of the way Daddy was taking all the attention away from her because the minute he walked out of the room she started giving us a lecture. She said the stove had exclusive built-in food guide dials with the right setting for eighty-two main dishes. She told us not to touch the dials because she didn't want us to tear it up.

Mama said the electric stove represents progress. I agree that it will be neat not having to go outside during winter to get wood, but the wood stove was worth all the inconvenience. Things will never be the same again. The old wood stove gave the kitchen an atmosphere of family. I will miss putting a couple pieces of wood in the stove to heat up the coffee pot while I wash dishes.

Grandmama always said drinking coffee will make me black, so I am not permitted to drink it. I slipped and drank it, and then I checked my face over carefully, but I never did see any changes to my complexion. I'm chocolate anyway, so I guess being a little darker shade won't matter. I'll miss the old stove, but most of all, I'll miss turning my rear end toward the fire, pulling up my dress, and letting the heat strike my bare flesh. Now *that* was living at its finest.

No, life will not be the same.

***

Noah and Gabriel had an awful fight today. It wasn't actually a fight, but more a test of wills. Gabriel always picks fights with Noah. If Noah refuses to let him have his way, Gabriel will smack him. He will do it in front of anybody. Mama told Noah that he needs to stop Gabriel, but Noah refuses to fight him. Noah took the Charles Atlas bodybuilding course. He's afraid he'll hurt Gabriel since Gabriel is so frail. Noah says Gabriel is quick-tempered, but Mama says Gabriel picks his victims. He doesn't fight anybody else in the neighborhood—just Noah.

Well, today Gabriel pulled a knife on Noah. Mama said that was the straw that broke the camel's back. It was high time that Gabriel learned once and for all that he couldn't beat Noah.

Daddy moved the dining room suit into the living room. He gave Gabriel and Noah each a hickory switch. He signaled for them to begin their battle. Noah backed around the room in a circle. Lunging to hit Noah, Gabriel kept advancing on him. He struck at Noah. Noah dodged. He lashed at Noah again. Noah dodged. Gabriel aimed carefully. Noah stared into his eyes, trying to anticipate his next move. Gabriel was faster than Noah. This time the stick connected, wrapping around Noah's body.

Gabriel jerked it loose. He hit Noah again, again, and again. Noah's eyes became blazes of fire. He returned Gabriel's licks with more power than Gabriel ever could have. Gabriel was stunned. Noah had never hit him back. Tears trickled down Noah's cheeks. He threw down his switch, balled up his fist, and knocked Gabriel's lights out. That's when I left the room.

I thought there had to be a better way to change Gabriel's behavior than to have two brothers beat each other mercilessly. Where did Mama get her ideas? From Hitler?

***

It's that time of year again. Every winter Mama and Daddy give Noah, Gabriel, and me a fat dose of Castor Oil to clean out our systems. Matthew is lucky; he's too young. Mama says this way we won't come down with a cold. I'd rather be sick.

I hate Castor Oil. It's so nasty. Grandmama says the medicine that tastes the worst to you is also the best for you. I don't know which is worse, smelling the Castor Oil or tasting it. The very thought of it makes me break out in a cold sweat.

Grandmama believes in Castor Oil almost as much as she believes in God. She starts the ritual off by taking a dose first to show us children that it's not that bad. Does she think I'm crazy? I took the stuff last year and the year before that!

The procedure is always the same. Mama and Daddy heat up a bottle and give each of us three tablespoons full. It takes every grownup in the house to give me my dose. Daddy and Cousin Ruth hold my hands behind my back, Grandmama holds my nose, and Mama shoves the spoon into my mouth. Grandmama says if I swallow the Castor Oil fast, I won't taste it. Slow or fast, it's still nasty.

When the torture is over, they give me an orange soda to drink. That's supposed to kill the taste, but it never does. The rest of the day I belch up Castor Oil. I'll be glad when I get grown. I will never take another dose of Castor Oil again! As a matter of fact, when I get rich, I'm going to buy up all the Castor Oil in the world and lock it in a warehouse. I'll give it to children when they grow up so they can give it to their parents.

Now that would be fun!

CHAPTER 4
EYE OPENER—1955

Having a baby brother can be fun, but sometimes it's nothing but trouble. For one thing, Mama says that now that Matthew is born we have to take more responsibility. Gabriel told her he didn't think that was fair, because he hadn't wanted another brother. Mama explained that sometimes having a baby was like the coming of a hurricane, flood, or tornado—unplanned and unwanted. When those occurrences upset our regular schedules, we all have to pitch in and help.

Mama also explained that a family is really a small community. She said she and Daddy are the rulers, and we are their citizens. To be loyal citizens, we must obey the laws. Noah asked if we could vote on the laws. Mama said she and Daddy were dictators. If we didn't obey the laws our heads would be chopped off. We knew she was teasing about chopping off our heads, but we still had to obey the rules.

Daddy explained that everybody in the family would have responsibilities that they must carry out without being reminded every day. Mama and Daddy would work outside the home, and we would have specific chores to do at home. One of our main duties was to take Matthew to the babysitter every morning. Mama would cook breakfast, pack Matthew's baby bag, and leave for work. I saw to it that everybody ate breakfast and didn't leave any unnecessary supplies at home.

Noah and Gabriel were responsible for carrying my books and the baby bag. I carried Matthew. He's devoted to me. I hate to leave him when it's time to drop him off. He holds on to me and cries frantically as I tear myself away from him. It breaks my heart. I never knew I could love a little baby so much. I might have one one day when I'm married.

A baby would enjoy playing on the beach in California.

***

Mama received some news today that should have been good news to the entire family, but it didn't make me happy. Members of the Monroe Board of Education voted to increase substitute teacher pay fifty percent. Mama had announced that it wasn't worth teaching for the amount of money she received, because she always had to keep her hair done and her clothes prepared. In disgust, she had mentioned quitting, but now I guess I'm stuck having her as a substitute teacher.

Don't get me wrong, she's a good teacher, but the only real whipping I ever received in school was the one *she* gave me. It was last year when I was in Mrs. Baylor's class. Mrs. Baylor had headaches every day, and sometimes she would tell us to go play outside while she rested her head on her desk. She would be absent for a week or two. Then she would return only to be absent again for several weeks. Finally, she didn't come back at all. We had several substitute teachers until Mama was hired to finish the term.

I knew Mama was a no-nonsense person, but I wanted to act the same way Alice and Shirlie did. One of Mama's rules was no talking in the classroom during study time. To get around the rule, we started meeting in the cloakroom. Then Mama instituted a new rule: no congregating in the cloakroom. Since we all go to church, we decided that we would have to congregate in large groups in order to break that rule. Therefore, we decided to meet in groups of two's and four's. We really didn't have anything to talk about. It was just something to do. Mama had noticed what was happening, so she warned me at home to stay out of the cloakroom.

The next day while we were waiting to go to lunch Shirlie winked her eye at me. That meant "meet me in the cloakroom." She got up and went in the room first. I waited two or three minutes. Then Ralph, Leon, and Charles came in. I realized there were too many of us in the room.

"Why did you guys come in here?" I asked, not waiting for an answer. "We were in here first."

Before they could answer, Mama entered the room.

"Didn't I tell you to stay out of this cloakroom?" She asked, looking right at me.

She was holding a black, leather strap in her hand. Actually, it was the fan belt from a car. That's what some teachers used if they didn't have a paddle (The Board of Education). Seeing the strap, we ran for the cloakroom door. Everybody got out except me. I felt the strap sting my legs several times. Then she moved aside enough to let me leave the cloak room. I cried from then on until time to go home. The licks hadn't hurt me that badly. I had been embarrassed.

When I reached home, I went straight to my bedroom and stayed there until it was time to eat supper. After supper, I did my homework and went to bed. I didn't want to face Mama because I knew I had been wrong. Mama confronted me anyway. She came into my room and sat on the side of the bed.

"Sit up," she said. "I want to talk with you."

I obeyed.

"Do you know why I whipped you today?" She asked.

"I broke your cloakroom rule," I replied.

"That's true," she said. "But that's not the only reason why I whipped you."

I was confused.

"Why do you think you were the only one who was trapped in the cloakroom with me?"

"I wasn't fast enough," I answered.

"That's not true," she said. "I deliberately let them get out."

"That's not fair!" I said in anger.

"I didn't say it was," she said. "But let me ask you something. Was it fair what you did to me today?"

"I didn't do anything to you," I said defensively.

"Think for a moment," she cautioned. "What did you do to me?"

"I disobeyed you." I answered.

"Not only that, but you also disrespected me. I'm your mother. If you don't respect me, how can I expect other people's children to respect me?"

What she was saying made sense to me.

"I'm not asking you to be as good as everyone else. I'm asking you to be better. Is it fair? Probably not, but I need your support. All the students will be looking at your behavior and how I react to it. I had to make an example of you today. If I had not, my authority would have been undermined. I would have lost every student's respect in that room if I had allowed you to break the rules and go unpunished."

Mama paused and patted my leg. "I made believers out of them today. They know if I'll whip you, my own daughter, I'll whip them."

She stood up from the edge of my bed and said, "Well, that's over now. Good night, sweetie." Then she bent and kissed my forehead. "Pleasant dreams."

"Good night, Mama," I answered, pulling the cover over my head, as one of Daddy's ghost stories popped into my mind.

It was going to be a long night.

***

I couldn't wait for the newspaper to come last Friday. East Parkway Elementary School's honor roll was in the paper. It's not published but every six weeks. I guess they only put it in when no one else wants the space. There it was—"Fifth Grade"—my name headed the list followed by Thomas Brown, Edna Goosby, Nedra Smith, Jonathan Gay, Brian Mathis, and Chris White.

Mama always does something special for me every time I make the honor roll. It's not something spectacular, because I always make the honor roll! Nevertheless, I do get to buy or do something I really want to do. For my gift I chose to see *From here to Eternity.* I like Burt Lancaster's rugged good looks and Montgomery Clift's boyish charm. But my favorite part is when Deborah Kerr and Frank Sinatra make love on the beach.

I can't wait to get to California.

***

It's spring cleaning time!

Usually I don't like doing housework, but spring cleaning is one event I look forward to. The house looks and smells like a new place. Every year we do the same things, so everybody knows his responsibility. Grandmama, Mama, and I do the curtains. The first thing we do is to take down the lace curtains in the living room. If the weather is cloudy, we postpone the curtain washing. Starch works better on a sunny day. The curtains are washed, starched, and put on curtain stretchers.

When the curtains dry, we remove them from the stretchers and rehang them.

While we are busy with the curtains, Noah and Gabriel are busy stripping the beds and taking the mattresses outside to sun. They also place newspaper down on the back porch and empty the contents of each pillow on a different newspaper. They are sunned for several hours. While the mattresses and pillows are being sunned, each person selects a room to wash the windows. We're also responsible for cleaning the windowsills and removing any cobwebs found in the room. I selected the room I shared with Grandmama, because I wanted it to be spotless.

When I went behind the head of my bed to check for cobwebs, I noticed some folded up sheets of paper on the floor that must have fallen from the bed when Noah and Gabriel removed the mattress. I hide things between my bed and the wall. Whatever it was, I decided, must not have been too important or else I would have remembered to remove it before spring cleaning.

I opened the sheets of paper. I had to muffle my laughter. The papers were a letter I had received last year from Jeremiah. I really had had a crush on him, but he laughed at me when I told him I wanted to move to California and become a movie star like Marilyn Monroe.

I could never love him. I would have to stay in Georgia, work at a job I hate, and have five or six kids. I actually heard him say he wants six kids! I have to be free to go to California and live on the beach. That is my heart's desire. The letter was sweet but so childish, and I wanted to be anything but childish.

My dearest love,
I was sitting at home thinking of you, so
I decided to write some poetry:

It began:

Apples on the table
Peaches on the shelf
Baby I'm tired of sleeping by myself.

I giggled. At eleven I wasn't thinking about getting married.

He continued:
I was sitting on the
back porch eating some fish.
I thought about you and
almost ate the dish.
Now that was silly I thought.
Greens in the garden got to be cropped.
Those other boys you're loving got to be stopped.

"Who is he talking about?" I wondered. I didn't have a boyfriend. I'd never had one. Yuk! That was a sloppy thought. I smiled at my own joke. When I read the part that said:
I love you on the bottom
I love you on the top
I love you better than
A hog loves slop.

I knew we had nothing in common. Didn't he know that girls didn't want to be compared to hogs? Anyway, it was a silly letter. I was glad Noah and Gabriel had not found that stupid letter. They would have teased me until I cried. I would have had to hear about that dumb letter for the rest of my life. Yes, it was a stupid letter from a stupid boy. That's all it was. I tore the letter up and put the pieces in my pocket for safe keeping. I would throw it away later. Instead of looking for cobwebs, I decided to wash windows. I scrubbed the panes cheerfully as the sounds of sea gulls and surging waves drowned out reality.

***

Sometimes I think I'm going crazy. My dreams are so colorful and life-like. Last week I dreamed I had been left in a deserted town. After searching for hours for humans, I began to cry uncontrollably. When I woke up, my face was wet with tears. This sort of thing happens constantly. Sometimes I tell Noah and Gabriel about my dreams, but they don't believe me. They say everybody dreams in black and white.

Friday night a strange thing happened. I dreamed that Mrs. Baylor had died. Her husband had the wake at his home. The casket was placed near a double window that was decorated with pink sheers. The sheers floated gently over the casket, giving the room a mystical appearance. I was in line waiting my turn to view the body. I finally inched my way to the casket. When I looked in, Mrs. Baylor had a peaceful look on her face. I thought I saw her smile.

I had never seen her with makeup on. I noticed the pink shroud she was wearing matched the pink sheers. She looked like an angel. I wanted to kiss her good-bye, but I was scared. I don't know how long I stood staring at her, but someone touched me lightly on the shoulder and courteously reminded me that other family members, friends, and students were in line to view the body.

The touch seemed to have awakened me. I sat up in bed, frightened. I remembered I hadn't kept my promise to go see her again. I prayed that I had been dreaming. Mrs. Baylor couldn't be dead. Promises are made to be kept, not broken. Daddy says a man is only as good as his word. I had to keep my promise to Mrs. Baylor. I tried to go back to sleep, but I couldn't. I tossed and turned until morning, hoping to hear news that she was still alive.

Bad news travels fast. Saturday morning when I went to the breakfast table, everyone had solemn looks on their faces. I can't explain how, but I knew that Mrs. Baylor was dead. Mama set a bowl of cheese grits on a trivet. She placed the bacon on the left side of the centerpiece. She returned to the kitchen to bring out the eggs and biscuits. She placed them next to the strawberry jam and butter. Then she sat down. Daddy blessed the food.

Each of us children said a Bible verse.

Gabriel said, "Father, forgive them for they know not what they do." That was his old standby.

I repeated my favorite verse: "Blessed are they that believe in Him."

Noah said, "Jesus wept." He always tried to say a short verse so he could get down to the business at hand.

Mama cleared her throat. I thought she was going to say a verse of scripture, but she didn't. Instead she said very bluntly, "Mrs. Taylor died last night."

That was the news I hadn't wanted to hear, but in a way I was relieved. I could breathe a sigh of relief. I wasn't insane after all. My dreams had meaning. To my surprise, I didn't feel any grief for Mrs. Baylor. I just felt numb.

"I knew she was dead," I replied.

"How?" Mama asked.

"I dreamed it last night."

"That's nonsense," Mama argued. "You must have heard Mrs. Williams when she came down here and told me this morning."

"I didn't," I protested. "I actually saw her death in my dreams."

Noah and Gabriel laughed at me.

"Who are you now?" Daddy teased. "Mother Lora, the fortune teller."

I jumped up from the table in tears.

"Come back to this table now and eat your breakfast," Daddy said.

"Oh let her go, George," Mama said. "Give her some time alone. She's just lost someone very dear to her."

I went to my room and cried. I wasn't crying about Mrs. Baylor. I was crying because no one had believed me or was interested in what I was saying. Instead, they made fun of me. There's so much I have bottled up inside me—things that are gnawing at my insides. Take for instance the sexual dreams I've had over and over again. Sometimes the picture flashes in my mind when I'm in school, at home, shopping with Mama, or anywhere. I see myself doing something to someone that I'm ashamed of doing. All I see is a body outline.

I want to tell Mama, but I'm afraid she'll blame me. I don't know what is happening to me or has happened to me. I just want to know. There's so much I could tell them. Like the time I saw Jesus. I didn't actually see his face, but I did see Him. He was standing up high, looking down at me. He didn't say anything to me. He just looked at me. I looked straight into His face, but I couldn't see anything. I was blinded by the glow that surrounded His head. I covered my eyes with my hands. When I opened my eyes later, He had gone. Everyone would just call me a liar or make jokes about my wild imagination. From now on I'll keep my dreams and visions to myself. That way no one can make fun of me. It wouldn't hurt them to try to understand me just a little.

It's lonely being different.

***

Cousin Ruth took me to Mrs. Baylor's funeral today. I wish I could say I was overwrought with grief, but I can't. The whole affair was like a rerun of a bad movie I had seen before. It was exactly like the dream I had. The only variation was the singing. The mourners were singing "Nearer My God to Thee, Nearer to thee. Even though there be a cross that raiseth me." The harmonic singing gave the funeral a ritual atmosphere.

There Mrs. Baylor was just like in the dream, dressed in a pink shroud in a pink casket in the living room. An unexpected breeze from the raised window even ruffled the pink sheers, sending them floating back and forth above the casket, coming to rest on her face. I moved the sheers from her face and whispered a good-bye. That was the end of that. She was dead and there was nothing I could do.

I didn't want to go to the graveyard. I'd never seen a casket lowered into the ground and covered with dirt. I wondered whether Mrs. Baylor was afraid of the dark. I hadn't asked her whether or not she believed in God. All teachers went to church. They had to if they wanted to keep their jobs, but that didn't mean anything. Lots of people do things they don't believe in. I wish she would come to me in a dream and tell me what it feels like to be dead. I have often wondered.

***

Mama and I went shopping today. I knew she was trying

to cheer me up. Life hasn't been the same since Mrs. Baylor died. Daddy said I should be glad that she's gone to a better home. All her pain is over. I'm glad she's gone to live with God, but I miss her so much. Daddy says I'm just being selfish.

Mama tried so hard to keep my mind off her. I really enjoy these walks with Mama. It's like we become different people. She's more like a best friend while we're out walking. I get to see the carefree, cheerful, and sometimes naughty side of her. I like that side of her.

Today she told me a story about Aunt Judy. She swears it's the gospel truth. Mama said the sheriff was up for reelection, so he decided to campaign in the colored community. Most politicians overlooked the colored people's votes or took them for granted. Sheriff Parson decided he would be different. Yes, he wanted to be reelected, and he wanted to win by a landslide. He knew the way to do it. He had always heard that all colored people loved chicken and barbecue ribs. He would broil so much meat until everyone would think the town was on fire.

Sheriff Parson executed his plan. He even had a country band perform. The crown was unbelievable. Old men, young men, light colored women, coal colored women, and jovial children loitered around eating barbecue. Dogs and stray cats fought over discarded bones. Eating was interrupted only long enough to shout, "Yes, sir" when Sheriff Parson asked then if they would support him.

The longer he talked, the more food the crowd ate. When Sheriff Parson finished his speech, he walked through the crowd kissing babies and indulging in meaningless conversation. At the end of the day he went home exhausted but sure of the colored folks votes. He counted votes in his head and smiled triumphantly.

Two weeks passed and election day arrived. Sheriff Parson

awoke early, dressed in his Sunday suit and went to the polls. He cast his vote and went home to wait for his victory. To his dismay, his opponent won the election. In fact, it was the biggest landslide in the history of Monroe County. He was sure a mistake had been made, but a recount showed the reports had been accurate. He was no longer sheriff.

Two weeks later Station WKFM advertised an appreciation barbecue to be given by ex-sheriff Parson for all the people who had voted for him. The invitation was sent out every thirty minutes throughout the day. During spiritual hour, it was made every fifteen minutes. That's because all the colored people listened to the colored DJ. That was the only time they got to hear gospel music.

Sheriff Parson scheduled the barbecue for the following Saturday. The crowd was twice as large as the first had been. He hired a local colored band to play. A scratchy voice cried the blues over the PA system. Barbecue ribs and chicken left greasy marks on jovial faces. Everyone was having a wonderful time. Sheriff Parson was even praised for giving the barbecue after losing the election.

As one old man put it, "No sir, Sheriff Parson was not a sore loser. He was even good to colored people."

After hours of carousing and stuffing their mouths, Sheriff Parson signaled the band to stop playing. He waved his hand to silence the crowd. Anticipation filled the air.

"Good evening, my friends," Sheriff Parson began.

The crowd cheered.

"I am so delighted to see so many of you here."

The crowd cheered again.

"I started out here with you. Therefore, I thought it proper to end here with you."

The crowd drowned him out.

"Wait, please let me speak." His voice was cracking. "I came here today to tell you what I think of you."

"Tell us! Tell us!" Coached someone from the crowd.

At that point, Sheriff Parson grabbed the mike, put his mouth close to it and shouted, "A nigger ain't shit!"

It was great to see Mama laughing. She said the story was funny, but it teaches a lesson about human nature. Mama said people will promise you one thing and do something different. According to Mama, we should never trust anybody completely, because no one is completely on your side. Expect the best, but be prepared for the worst. I'll try to remember her advice.

***

We took Cousin Ruth to Albany State College today. She plans to become a nurse. She should make a good nurse because she has a heart of gold. The only problem is she's not very bright. To use Grandmama's expression, her bread is not done in the middle. She will know what she wants to do, but she will let someone else talk her into doing something she never planned nor wanted to do. Nevertheless, Grandmama said everybody deserves a chance to make his own mistakes.

I hope she becomes a good nursing student because she has been good to me, not all the time, but most of the time. There was that one time when she took me to the fair and talked me into riding the ferris wheel. The first few rounds were fun. Then the ferris wheel stopped to take on more passengers. We were at the top.

Cousin Ruth looked at me and said, "I could push you out of this ferris wheel, and everyone would think you fell."

"Stop teasing, "I said, trying not to panic.

"I really could kill you and get away with it," she said.

The dazed look in her eyes told me she was serious until she started laughing.

"I was just joking," she said.

I forced a smile and gripped the bar with all my might just in case she decided to try to kill me.

I haven't ridden a ferris wheel since, and I don't ever intend to ride in another one as long as I live.

I never mentioned the incident to anyone, but I heard Grandmama telling Mama that Cousin Ruth had threatened her. Grandmama had said that Cousin Ruth had described in explicit detail how she could smother her at night. Mama said she would put Cousin Ruth out, but Grandmama didn't agree. She thought Cousin Ruth was trying to frighten her into giving her money. Grandmama never said whether or not she gave Cousin Ruth money. I do know they shared the same room until Cousin Ruth went off to college.

***

Life was a little different after Cousin Ruth went to college, but we soon settled into a new routine without her. Our lives were changed again soon, because she called home for Mama and Daddy to come to her college and bring her home. At first they thought she was sick or had been dismissed because of bad grades. I thought grades were the culprit because Cousin Ruth hadn't been the best student in school. Although she was nice, I always thought she was missing a few screws.

Mama said she was just naïve. She would give anyone the shirt off her back, and if that wasn't enough, she trusted everyone she met. I remember the time she became friends with a lady she had nothing in common with. Instead of coming home when she got off from work, she would stop by this woman's house. As time passed, Mama realized that Cousin Ruth was always trying to borrow money from her.

Now, Cousin Ruth did not pay rent and didn't buy groceries

unless she wanted something special to eat. Yet she never had money to buy her personal items. Mama questioned her about what she was doing with her money. She finally admitted that she had loaned it to her friends. Mama told her that they were taking advantage of her kindness. She blew up at Mama and accused her of not wanting her to have any friends. Mama told her that was not true. She said it hurt her to see someone she cared about being used.

Cousin Ruth promised Mama that she would not lend any more money to anyone else. Mama said if she had money she wanted to give away, she could give it to her. At least it would be spent in the house where Cousin Ruth lived.

For two weeks Cousin Ruth kept her promise. She came home promptly at six-thirty. Then on a Friday night there was a knock at the front door. Mama wasn't expecting company that late so she called Daddy and told him to answer the door. When Daddy opened the door, Louise greeted him with a big smile. She asked for Cousin Ruth. It seemed she had a cousin with her who was visiting from New York, and she had promised her that she would introduce her to her best friend Ruth.

When they seated themselves in the living room, Daddy excused himself to finish the work he was doing in the kitchen. Mama soon followed. I was watching "Have Gun, Will Travel", and I wasn't about to give that up for anyone. Nevertheless, I didn't get to enjoy the show because I was distracted by Louise's questions. She pretended to be watching the television, but it was obvious she was more interested in Mama's household items that she was in any television program.

She asked Cousin Ruth all kinds of questions in what she thought were clever ways. At one time she said, "Oh, what beautiful lamps! Turn on the light so I can see their true beauty."

Cousin Ruth turned on the lamp as Louise wrote something on a scrap of paper. I got up and turned the light off. They watched the show in silence. Sometime later she asked, "What kind of television is that? The picture is so clear."

"A Motorola," Cousin Ruth answered.

Louise wrote that down.

Later, she looked at me and said, "I'll bet you like to listen to music. What kind of stereo is that?"

I didn't answer her. Instead, I gave her my "get lost" look. I had learned if from Mama. I must have gotten my message across because she didn't say another word until "Have Gun, Will Travel" went off.

Louise arose from the sofa and said, "Well, it's time for us to leave. I just wanted you to meet my cousin before she leaves for New York tomorrow."

While Cousin Ruth was walking with them to the car, I went to the kitchen to tell Mama what I had observed.

"Mama," I said. "Miss Louise didn't come here to introduce her cousin to us."

"What makes you say that?" Mama asked.

"She came to see what you have in the house."

"How do you know that?"

"Because she wrote down the brand names of as many items as she could," I replied.

"Why would she do that?" Mama asked.

"I don't know," I answered. "But I saw her. I did."

Mama looked at me in disbelief. She was as puzzled as I was, and she's usually up on things.

Daddy ended the conversation by making a joke out of the incident. "There you go again with your wild imagination."

I returned to the living room grumbling to myself, "I know what I saw."

A month later Mama and Daddy got a notice about an overdue bill on a loan. Mama threw the bill away because she knew she didn't owe anyone any money. Several days later they received a call from the credit manager telling them they needed to pay their overdue loan. If they did not, he would send someone to pick up the furniture they had used as collateral.

By this time Mama was fuming! She told the manager she had never been to his company before. He told Mama and Daddy to come downtown so they could straighten out the matter. As it turned out, the lady had borrowed money in Mama's name. The manager said he realized Mama hadn't been the person who borrowed the money, because the lady had been tall, slender, and fair complexioned. In contrast, Mama is short, stout, and dark-skinned. The manager was convinced he had been the victim of fraud. The only thing they could not explain was how they got Mama's social security number.

I will always believe until my dying day that Cousin Ruth had given it to them because the description the manager gave perfectly described Louise's cousin from New York. If Cousin Ruth could be so gullible in one situation, there was no telling what mess she had gotten herself into. We soon found out.

Mama and Daddy went to Albany State College to bring her home, but she had been getting her mail at a mailbox, so they were unaware that she was not living in a dorm. That's where they had left her when she entered school. The Dean gave Mama Cousin Ruth's city address and directions on how to find where she was living. Mama and Daddy found the house easily. It was just like many of the houses at home. We called them shotgun houses. You can stand in the living room and look straight through into the dining room, from the dining room into the kitchen, and from the kitchen to the outdoors. On the left side of the house three bedrooms emptied into a living room, dining room, and kitchen. There was no place to hide in such a compact house.

As we drove into the yard, I could see Cousin Ruth standing on the porch holding a screen door halfway open. She had a worried smile on her face. Nevertheless, I could tell she was happy to see us. She hugged each one of us as we entered the porch. I had missed her so much, especially the chocolate candy she had always brought me.

Mama was the first to speak. "Child, what are you doing here?" She asked in a disturbed voice.

"I got married," Cousin Ruth answered.

"Why didn't you tell somebody?"

Looking away from Mama, Cousin Ruth said, "I thought you'd try to stop me."

Daddy didn't say a word. He slapped his thigh with his hat. He always did that when he was disgusted.

"Well, where is he now?" Mama asked.

"He's working."

"Who is this man?"

Before Cousin Ruth could answer, Mama continued her interrogation.

"How did you meet him?"

Cousin Ruth led us inside and pointed to a picture of a man who looked old enough to be her father.

"Good Lord!" Mama cried in disbelief. "You sure can pick a man! This man is old enough to be *my* daddy!"

By this time Cousin Ruth could hold back her tears no more.

"Uncle George, Aunt Candy…I want to go home. He's mean to me."

"What do you consider mean?" Daddy asked.

"You know, mean. Before I married him he used to take

me to the movies. He would give me romantic cards, send me roses, and feed me breakfast in bed. Now he won't do any work around the house. He says that's what women are for—To cook, wash and iron, and fulfill her man's sexual needs."

"And you take that?" Mama asked.

"What else can I do?" Cousin Ruth asked helplessly. "He took my clothes and locked them up."

"Where?" Daddy asked, showing some genuine concern for the first time.

Cousin Ruth's speedy reply was that the clothes were in a trunk in the bedroom, and her husband was the only one with the key.

She led us into the bedroom and pointed to a ragged trunk. In her fear, she had never touched it before.

Mama took one look at the trunk and burst out laughing.

"Is this what's holding your clothes?" She asked.

I could see she was amused.

"You don't need a key to get in here."

With those words, she began to lift the sides of the trunk off its frame. The trunk had no bottom in it! We all laughed hysterically. Mama said Cousin Ruth had been the victim of mind control.

"Get your things and lets get out of here before he comes home," Mama said. "Apparently you're married to a fool and you can never predict what a fool will do."

That was the end of Cousin Ruth's formal education, and that was the end of her marriage too. Harold, her husband, came to the house once to try to get her to take him back. He didn't get to talk to Cousin Ruth though because Mama slipped her out the back door. She went through the bushes and down the highway.

I heard them say he shouldn't be permitted to get near her because if did he might want to rootwork her. They hoped he didn't have any of her hair because if he did he could run her crazy and make her do anything. A person had to always be careful with her hair. When my hair shedded, Mama told me to never throw it outdoors. If a bird found someone's hair and put it in several nests, that person could lose her mind. It would be an accident, but the person would be crazy just the same. I heard that a person could do the same thing with a picture. I guess Harold didn't know how to cast a spell on anybody, because Cousin Ruth soon stopped talking about him. I suppose he hadn't wanted her as badly as he had pretended, because he never came looking for her again.

***

Mama's back at home now. She went to Daytona Beach, Florida to stay with Aunt Judy while she had her baby. Until now, Mama had always been able to tolerate Uncle Steve, but now she finds him totally despicable. Mama said if she had not been at the hospital herself and seen what happened, she would never have believed anyone else. The whole thing was incredible.

Mama said Aunt Judy went into labor around twelve o'clock on Sunday night. She and Uncle Steve called her obstetrician, who told her to meet him at the hospital when her pains became fifteen minutes apart. They followed the doctor's instructions carefully.

A nurse was waiting for Aunt Judy at the emergency entrance. Mama and Uncle Steve helped Aunt Judy into a wheelchair and rushed her into the delivery room. Her doctor checked her carefully. Everything checked out normal, but her pelvis wasn't dilating. She stayed in the delivery room all night. When the baby failed to come, she was assigned to a room.

The next day Aunt Judy was given shots to speed up her delivery. Still no baby came. By late afternoon, Mama said Aunt Judy was no longer coherent. Several doctors were called in to diagnose her problem. The complications came as a surprise because she had had a normal pregnancy. Mama thought that maybe that fall she took in the grocery store had something to do with her problem. Aunt Judy had sued the store, but Mama said money's no good if you're six feet under.

Something had gone terribly wrong. She was in a life and death struggle. Mama said she will never be able to forget the moment the doctor called her and Uncle Steve aside for a conference. Mama said the doctor in a matter-of-fact voice told them that Aunt Judy had only a fifty-fifty chance to live. You would have thought he was just giving them the weather forecast. Uncle Steve had become distraught and begged the doctor to tell him what to do.

"You can pray," the doctor had told him.

Uncle Steve had been surprised by the doctor's answer. He didn't know whether it was professional for a doctor to advise him to pray. After all, he was not a praying man, but he decided it couldn't do any harm. Nevertheless, he escaped to a private spot to pray.

Aunt Judy struggled to birth her baby as a nurse stayed by her side all night. By morning doctors had decided that she would not be able to birth the baby. Mama and Uncle Steve were called in for an update on Aunt Judy's condition. Mama said as she looked upon Aunt Judy's comatose body, the doctor told them that both Aunt Judy and the baby could not be saved.

To Mama's chagrin, Uncle Steve had blurted out, "Save my baby."

Of course, Aunt Judy's life was saved. Uncle Steve was

disappointed and made no effort to hide it. Aunt Judy had later revealed to Mama that even though she could not speak or open her eyes, she had been aware of what was going on around her. She had heard Uncle Steve offer her life for the unborn child. The marriage was over. When she got better, she had a hysterectomy. Uncle Steve told her she was no longer a woman. He would fulfill his desires somewhere else. He had desecrated their marriage. She would come home to Georgia as soon as she was strong enough.

***

Aunt Judy has left Uncle Steve. She won her lawsuit against the grocery store where she fell. Most of her money was put into a savings account; the rest was used to buy a house. By Aunt Judy's description, the house has everything she needs. The living room has a cathedral ceiling supported by glass walls on the east side. Large evergreens are placed strategically around the room to give it a tropical atmosphere. A calm, welcoming mood announces that the owner is at peace with herself. If a person likes antiques, Aunt Judy's home is the place to visit. A Duncan Fyfe dining room set, a grandfather clock, and an 1830's sofa announce to visitors that Aunt Judy has exquisite taste (I recently added exquisite to my vocabulary).

Having to brag about her new home wasn't the only reason Aunt Judy came to visit. She brought her dog Sparkle to live with us. She loves Sparkle, but he chews on her furniture. To keep him from being put to sleep, Mama said he could live with us.

Daddy built him a little house in the back yard, but he wouldn't go near it. Every day he would go to the curb and sit. He would not even leave the driveway entrance to eat his meals. Gabriel and I took turns taking his food to him. Noah said if he didn't have enough sense to eat, he ought to starve to death.

Sparkle didn't starve to death. Instead, we suspect he died of a broken heart. Every time he saw a car that resembled Aunt Judy's, his eyes lit up and his tail wagged in anticipation. When the car failed to stop, he would lower his head and cry. Mama said dogs don't cry, but I actually saw tears in Sparkle's eyes. Eventually, he stopped eating. I went out one day and found him dead. He had grieved himself to death.

From Sparkle's death, I learned a valuable lesson about love. You should never abandon someone who's devoted to you. If you love somebody, that person needs to love you back. If they don't, your heart will ache. It will get weaker and weaker. One day it will just stop pumping, and you will die of a broken heart.

I pray that one day my dream lover will love me the way Sparkle loved Aunt Judy.

***

I didn't get my piano, but I'm still going to learn how to play music. The music teacher gave everyone in our class a test. It seemed stupid to me, but Mr. Moore said the test would identify people who have musical talent. All he did was to play different sounds, and we had to identify the instrument making the sounds.

When he finished scoring our tests, he told us who had passed and asked us what instrument we wanted to play. When he got to me, I told him I wanted to play the drums. He told me that only boys could beat drums. He suggested I play the clarinet. I didn't want to play the clarinet, but I wanted to be in the band. I also didn't have an instrument. He volunteered to let me use his. I accepted his offer because I knew Daddy wasn't going to buy me one. Gabriel is already in the band, and Mama and Daddy wouldn't be able to afford to pay for two instruments.

Does Benny Goodman play the clarinet?

***

Old Acid Tongue did it again. She picks a new student out every day to burn. Today was my lucky day. I wore the new dress Grandmama ordered for me from Belles Hess. I met the postman every day for six weeks! My dress is so pretty. It has a short cape that makes me think of Sherlock Holmes. I like to imagine myself living a mysterious life.

Well, anyway, I walked into Mrs. Pinkney's room eager to show off my beautiful red dress. As soon as I stepped into the room, Old Acid Tongue lit into me.

"How could your mother let you out of the house looking like that?" she asked.

I looked behind me. I thought she was talking to someone else, but she kept staring at me.

"I'm talking to you in the red dress!" she shouted.

I wanted to tell her that that was my dress, and I could wear any color I wanted. Besides, that wasn't just any old red dress. It was the dress my grandmama had ordered for me, and I had filled out the order form. I didn't say anything because I had seen her shake students for talking back to her. Whenever you try to explain yourself, you get deeper and deeper into a hole. Old Acid Tongue just pours more acid on you. I didn't want the school to burn down!

Good Lord, Mrs. Pinkney can fuss! She went on and on explaining why I shouldn't wear red. She even "for your own good" threw in a few extra colors: yellow, purple, and orange. She also cautioned me to stay away from some shades of brown.

According to Old Acid Tongue, I am chocolate and brown does not complement my color. Within a few minutes, she had eliminated four colors from my wardrobe.

I'll be glad when this school term comes to an end. I'll stay inside all summer and bleach my skin.

***

A colored lady was on the news in Alabama today. She was arrested for not giving her seat on a bus to a white man. Valdosta is no different from Montgomery. Colored people ride in the back of the bus and white folks ride in the front. I know because I've seen the buses downtown. Mama and Daddy never let us ride the bus. Before we got our car we walked everywhere we went.

Mama said we're as good as anybody else. She rode the bus once, and she said sixty year-old ladies stood up to let six and seven year-olds sit down. Mama said that was the last time she rode the city bus. Mama said she'd rather walk in dignity than ride in shame. I wonder why Mrs. Parks wouldn't give up her seat.

***

Tonight's dinner was a celebration. A colored lady named Marian Anderson sang at the Metropolitan Opera House. Daddy said that just proves that colored people can do anything they set their minds on doing. The trick is to practice, practice, practice, and never give up. Does that mean he's going to get me my piano? I still want to become a concert pianist. I need a piano so I can practice six or seven hours a day. Mama said colored people have to be ten times better than anybody else if they want to be successful.

Two glorious things happened today: Marian Anderson made history, and I learned how to spell Metropolitan.

***

I'm getting better on the clarinet. Its hard work, but I like a good challenge. I'm playing second chair, but I want to move up to first chair. Anything I'm a part of I like to be the best. I know Hester has been playing longer than I have, but I have it all figured out. If I practice twice as many hours as she does, I can get better than she is.

There's only one problem. I have to practice on the back porch. I haven't gotten past squeaking. Mr. Moore says I'm not sucking my reed enough. I also pinch the reed. The squeaking could be caused by the cold. There's no heat on the porch. I get cold, but I don't complain. I've read about starving artists. Most artists don't get famous until *after* they're dead. I don't want to die, but I'm willing to suffer for art.

***

Someone opened a club on the corner. Mama and Daddy are very upset. They say a white juke joint in a colored neighborhood spells trouble. Mama has four sons and Mrs. Lillian has six sons. They are worried about someone falsely accusing them of rape.

It's really free entertainment. This afternoon I saw ladies come outside and pull their panties down in broad daylight. They were not embarrassed or ashamed. Daddy and Mama were furious. They said that was just the type of thing they were talking about. They made us children go back into the house. Before we could go to bed tonight, we had to promise to ignore the people on the corner. I have to be truthful and admit that I'm going to have a hard time keeping my promise, because I didn't know people did some of the things I've seen those people do. Daddy said we have to look over them because they don't know any better. I think they do. I think they came into a colored neighborhood so their friends won't see them. Still, I'll pretend that Daddy's right and not say anything against them.

***

I hate the South! I can't wait until I'm old enough to move to California. Just the other day a man was arrested in Mangel's Clothing Store. Mama and I were shopping for my birthday gift. We were standing in line to pay for our goods. I was so excited about my new dress. Two policemen rushed in, grabbed the man, threw him to the floor, and handcuffed his hands behind his back. He could be heard asking, "What have I done?" as he was manhandled out the door. A clerk in the store explained to all the customers that the man had been arrested for "reckless eyeballing". I didn't understand the charges, but when I got home Daddy explained it to me.

Daddy said it's an unwritten law that a colored person is not supposed to look a white person straight in the eyes. In fact, whenever Daddy wanted a favor from a white person, he would cast his eyes downward and fold his arms nervously. He said white folks liked that. Mama always fussed at him about doing that. She said she'd "rather die the death of a polecat and stink her way to hell" before she'd play the "good ole' nigger" game. It was dangerous for a colored man to defy a white man, but she was a woman and women could do what men couldn't do. White men loved to fool around with colored women, so they were careful not to be too harsh if a woman was attractive.

I though the "reckless eyeballing" incident was bad enough, but today I read in the paper that a fourteen year-old boy from

Chicago had been killed in Mississippi because he said "Bye, baby" to a white woman in a grocery store. In Chicago he had white friends and was used to teasing, but he was in Money, Mississippi and he had made a deadly mistake. Some men dragged him from his cousin's grandfather's house and sped off into the night. Mama and Daddy called our family together for a meeting. Daddy said someone should have explained to the boy how to survive in the South. Mama insisted that he had a right to be a child, even in the South. Although they disagreed on how the Till boy should have acted, they both agreed that there was no woman in the world worth dying for.

When I pray tonight I'm going to ask God to take care of my brother Noah and to help him exercise good judgment. Noah is a stock boy at Butler's Shoe store. To borrow one of Mama's phrases: "He's putting his head on a chopping block and supplying the axe." He's dating a white sales clerk who also works at the store. It's a secret between him and me. Everyone thinks Sue is my friend. Whenever she calls the house, she asks to speak to me. If no one is around, I call Noah to the phone. Tomorrow I'm going to tell my brother that I'm not going to be his go-between anymore. If anything happens to him, I'd kill myself.

Besides, Daddy's already warned Noah and Gabriel about what happens to colored men when a white woman is discovered with them. They always holler rape and some poor colored man is hanged or burned to death. Daddy knows it for a fact because he saw a colored man burned to death when he was a teenager. Daddy said the man's family members were sharecroppers, and the owner's teenaged daughter fell in love with a Negro. The boy tried to stay away from her, but she followed him around. She always had something for him to do for her—chop wood, make a fire, take in groceries, move furniture around—anything so she could be near him. Daddy said after a while, the boy was madly in love with her too.

One day the couple decided to meet in the cotton field. Daddy said as far as he can remember all they did was talk. When she did not show up on time for dinner, her father sent her brother to find her. The couple was still out in the field talking when she heard her brother calling her. Afraid her brother would tell her father she was with a colored man, she started running toward him. As she ran though the cotton field, her arm struck the cotton bushes. When she reached her brother, he asked her what she had been doing out in the fields. She told him she had wanted some privacy. Her brother took one look at her scratched arms and said, "You're lying." She refused to say anything.

At home her family took her into the parlor and questioned her until she finally told them she had been in the field with the sharecropper's son. Daddy said it was rumored that her father beat her unmercifully that night and shipped her off to a relative in New Orleans. Anyway, she was never seen again. Daddy said just being alone with the colored man had made her a "fallen woman". In the South, a white woman was looked upon as an earthly angel, her father or husband's honor and pride. Her reputation had to be "beyond reproach" as Daddy explained it. Anything less was unacceptable. It didn't matter that the man had not raped the woman. Just being alone with him had been enough. He had a debt to pay. The colored man was doomed to die. Her father had to preserve his family's honor and dignity. If there were room for reasonable doubt, people would talk.

Daddy said his lynching was the social even of the week. The man was kept locked up in a shack until all the arrangements for his lynching could be made. Late at night deathly cries could be heard. Daddy said everyone suspected he was being tortured, but no one was ever brave enough to talk about it. They just performed their daily tasks, pretending nothing had happened.

Sunday was the day of the lynching. Daddy said people came from miles around to witness the event. Men, women, and children arrived in cars and wagons. Many brought picnic lunches. When the mob had satisfied its wrath, they tied the Negro to a pole, stacked bushes around his feet, and set it afire. With bloodshot eyes, the mob watched the flames creep up his legs. Smoke from the fire could be seen for miles. The stench of human flesh tainted the air. Inhuman sounds filled the air until life left his body. The crowd disbursed slowly, disappointed that the burning was over.

Daddy ended the meeting by telling Noah and Gabriel to be careful. How could they not be? He had scared the life out of all us, especially me. I'm scared for all the colored men who will die because their skin is black. To tell the truth, I guess I'm just plain scared.

***

Gabriel got a whipping today. He broke ten of Mama's plates. He didn't do it intentionally. He was training to be a plate spinner. Sunday night while we were watching the Ed Sullivan Show we saw a man spinning plates on sticks. He had ten plates going at the same time! Gabriel said that was what he wanted to do for the rest of his life. He wouldn't have to go to college, and he wouldn't have to get out of bed early in the morning. There were two things Gabriel hated: work and getting up early. I tried to keep Gabriel from practicing with Mama's plates, but he said anybody could spin plates. He had the whole situation figured out. He said it wouldn't matter if he broke the plates because they hadn't cost anything. Once a month Grandmama always buys a ten-pound sack of White Lily flour. Each time she buys a sack, Mr. Henry Buckle gives her a plate. When the sack is empty, Grandmama washes the sack and uses it for cloth. Sometimes she uses it for a dishrag too.

The plates may have been free, but Grandmama liked them. She had collected eight plates. We used them every day. The bought china is used for Sunday dinner. That's why Mama was angry. We were forced to use the Sunday china. Mama said she would buy more china to be used everyday. That way we wouldn't break her best china too.

***

My friend Deanna came to play with me today. We had an awful fight. After our fight, Mama said I can't play with her anymore. Mama told me to be polite to her if she shows up at our house again, but I must never ask to go play with her. According to Mama, if I don't go to her house her Mama won't let her come to our house.

I've always enjoyed playing with Deanna, but lately she's started getting on my nerves. I have dolls, tea sets, crayons, skates—all the toys I want. Deanna doesn't have any, so every time she comes to play with me she pretends to steal my toys. It's not that she doesn't get any toys. Everybody gets toys at Christmas. If a family doesn't have any money, the Salvation Army gives them toys. I know because we received tickets to go to the old veteran building to receive toys and fruit. I threw the toy away. It looked nice, but I could tell it had been repaired. I didn't want something someone else had used and thrown away, but I pretended to be thankful. There were some people in town thinking they had brought happiness to some poor,black children. It was Christmas, so I guess it was all right for me to lie, but the fruit basket was another thing! I ate all the oranges and gave my brothers the apples. I don't like apples.

Deanna has nine brothers and sisters, and they tear up their toys as soon as they get them. Mama said that's what you expect when you have a house full of children. I feel sorry for Deanna, but I can't let her take my toys home with her. Mine would get torn up too.

Usually, Deanna and I played until it was dark. I would ask Mama if I could walk her halfway home. She would caution me not to go too far and to be home before dark. I'd walk halfway home with Deanna. She'd turn around and walk me half the way back home. Then I'd turn around and walk her half the way home again. We'd take turns walking each other home until one of our mothers would call us to come home. Recently things changed. Deanna started grabbing a doll, teacup- -anything she could grab and run toward her house. Somehow I always managed to catch her. When I would catch her, she would grin, hand me the toy, and say she was just teasing. Today she did the same thing, but this time she took my baton. I ran her down and snatched my baton from her.

"Give me my baton," I demanded.

"I was just teasing," she said.

"No you were not," I yelled, surprised at my own bravery.

"Do you think I was trying to steal your stupid baton?"

I was scared, but I said, "You know that's what you were doing." Then I blurted out, "Deanna, you're a rogue!"

That's when she slapped me. I closed my eyes and lit into her. She threw me to the ground and sat on top of me. That's when Mama showed up. Thank God! She pulled Deanna off me and told her to go home and never ask to play with me again.

Mama and I had a long, serious talk tonight. She said she was glad Deanna had slapped me. That way Deanna had forced me into acting. Mama said I should have stood up to her a long time ago. She said if we had not fought today, she was about to do something herself. Mama said having book sense is fine, but nothing beats having common sense. According to Mama, friendship is based upon trust. If you can't trust someone, that person is not a true friend. She also said friendship should not be seen as a license to take advantage of someone. A friend should be trusted at all times, but that trust has to be earned. That person has to be a responsible human being and be responsible for his actions. Mama said Deanna had showed me that she could not be trusted and that she was not my friend.

"I won't always be around to pick you up every time someone knocks you down," Mama said. "God gave you a mind. Use it."

Of all the things Mama said, the words "common sense" stood out. I am not stupid. I have common sense. My common sense tells me that I don't want to play with Deanna anymore. She has been taking advantage of me, and I've been letting her. Not only has she been using me, but she has also been disrespecting me. Friends don't treat friends that way. Friendship is a gift that should be valued. Deanna does not value me or value our friendship. It's time to say good-bye to Deanna.

***

So many things seem to cloud up our lives. Mama and I don't go on as many Sunday walks as we used to, but when we do, they are special. Mama feels free to talk about her past, especially about her late father. From the memories that Mama has shared with me, I can tell he was a selfish, scheming person.

Mama said Granddaddy always liked to work out of town. He convinced Grandmama that he could make more money in Florida, but Mama said he never brought home any more money. When Uncle Roosevelt quit school, Granddaddy took him to Florida to work too. Mama said they were away for six weeks. When they returned home they were not speaking. Uncle Roosevelt told Grandmama that they were paid three dollars for the first week's work. He had been proud of his earnings and had wanted to hold onto the money himself. Granddaddy wouldn't hear of it. Each week he insisted Uncle Roosevelt hand over his money for safekeeping. He wanted to see the look on Grandmama's face when he handed her the money. To his disappointment, Granddaddy handed him only three dollars. He had spent all of Uncle Roosevelt's money except for his last week's wages! Uncle Roosevelt packed up all his belongings and moved to Detroit, Michigan.

Don't get the wrong idea. Mama didn't grow up in poverty. She states that point with pride, but she would have if it had not been for Grandmama. Grandmama took in washing and ironing. Sometimes she and Mama shelled pecans at night. They also tied greens at a local plant. Mama said cloth was cheap, and she knew how to sew. Grandmama was also a good seamstress so Mama had nice clothes. Mama laughed as she remembered that Grandmama always left a big hem in her dresses. That way Grandmama could let the hem down when Mama grew taller. The only problem was that the let out section was always a different color from the rest of the dress. Mama said it wasn't a catastrophe because most parents followed the same practice.

Mama opened up old wounds as she revealed to me how Granddaddy had betrayed Grandmama. Mama said Grandmama bore his infidelities with quiet dignity. However,

one time she heard a rumor that ruffled her feathers—
something extremely hard to do. Someone told Grandmama
that Granddaddy was buying groceries for a lady who lived a
few blocks down the street from their house. He didn't actually
go to the market and buy groceries for her. On his way home
with his groceries, he would stop by his girlfriend's house and
let her select the cut of meats she wanted. When Grandmama
heard the report, she became furious and said she was going
that instant to confront the woman. She was going to ask her
to leave her husband alone. Mama said she was only a teenager,
but she knew Grandmama shouldn't go to the woman and
disgrace herself. Mama said she begged Grandmama not to
do it, but she did it anyway. Mama said she will never forget
the humiliation and shame she felt as the woman taunted
Grandmama.

"Don't blame me if you can't keep your man home. Go
home and tell your husband not to come here."

Mama said Grandmama cried all the way home. Part of
that hurt still remains with her today. That's why Mama says
she doesn't trust men. In fact, she says she doesn't trust anyone.
She says that on any given day anyone can be betrayed by
someone he trusts. Everyone has a price. Some people are just
more expensive than others. Nevertheless, they *can* be bought.

Those little stories about her life were Mama's way of
teaching me the facts of life. Along with the tragedies, Mama
told me a funny but disgusting incident. Grandmama was
going through menopause and was having trouble with her
eyesight. Granddaddy had promised to spend more time at
home, so he thought up different schemes to leave the house.
On a Saturday night when he'd exhausted all his reasonable
excuses, he became desperate.

Mama said Grandmama and Granddaddy were sitting on

the back door steps when he jumped up yelling, "Scat, cat, scat!"

He continued to run down the alley and shout, "Scat, cat, scat," until he was completely out of sight.

"There was not and never had been a cat anywhere around," Mama said. "Papa had made his escape for the night."

Mama put her arms around my shoulders, and we walked on without exchanging words. There was no need for conversation. Mama had let me into her private world. Her betrayal, hurt, and embarrassment were my possessions too. I understood my mother better now. Her toughness was her safety net. Her doubts, her fears, her disgust, and her insecurity had become strengths to be admired. My mama is some tough lady. I hope I can grow up and be as strong as she is.

***

Summer is here and we children have nothing to do. That's what everyone was saying until I suggested we organize our own community band. Everyone laughed at my suggestion.

To my surprise, Gabriel said, "Why not? We have enough people playing instruments. "Daniel," he said, "you play drums. I play the trumpet and Baby Girl plays the clarinet."

"I play saxophone," Red interjected.

My idea was catching fire.

Daniel said, "It won't be a real band. We don't have any majorettes."

That's when I remembered Deanna.

"I'll ask Mama to let me play with Deanna again. If she says yes, I'll ask Deanna to march with us. She's angry with me, but she would never turn down a chance to march. She's proud of making the line."

"I'll get on the phone and call a few people," Red volunteered.

"Tell them to meet us in our vacant lot," Gabriel said.

In less than an hour we were lining up and preparing to give the neighbors a rendition of "Stars and Stripes Forever" they would never forget.

CHAPTER 5
LESSONS IN LIFE 1956

I could have been killed tonight, but Noah and Gabriel said I was exaggerating. They said I was in no danger, but you could have fooled me. Tonight should have been fun, but it turned into a nightmare. We go to Easter practice on Mondays, Wednesdays, and Fridays. We walk to practice. Mama doesn't go with us. She entrusts my safety to my brothers, but she doesn't know how much devilment they get me into. They constantly think up new pranks for us to pull. Tonight we carried out one of the pranks that we had been successful with last week.

As usual, we put rocks, empty Coke bottles, and stones in a discarded brown paper grocery bag and took the bag to church with us. We hid the bad behind the church pillar before we went inside to practice our speeches and songs. Inside the church we were angels, but on the street we were devils. As soon as practice was over, Gabriel retrieved the bag. As usual, all three of us selected the items we wanted to throw at houses on our way home.

It was already dark when we left the church, so we weren't afraid of being identified. I trudged along behind Noah and Gabriel eager to participate in our little game. That's all it was—a silly, old game. We would throw things at houses and run away before anyone saw us. We were careful to target a different house each time we carried out our little prank, but this time everything fell apart. We made the tragic mistake of hitting the same house we had hit on Monday night! As soon as the debris crashed into the door, a large, bedraggled man carrying a shotgun burst from the house, yelling, "Those damn, no good hoodlums! I'll kill'em! Everyone of'em!"

Noah and Gabriel took off running. I froze in my tracks. As the man trudged toward me, fear surged though my quivering body and perspiration flooded my face. What was I going to do? Then I saw it—an open sewer. I struggled desperately to get onto the sewer unseen and unheard. Once inside, I began to cry. I wanted Mama, but most of all, I wanted to tell on my brothers. They had run off and left me to be killed by a madman.

While I was crying, I could hear the man's footsteps echoing above me. His angry voice filled the air. Only now I could tell he was not alone. Other voices were engaged in lively conversation relating how they too had had doors dented and windows smashed. I knew I was in big trouble and had to get away anyway I could. I was afraid of snakes, frogs, and other night creatures, but I decided that being bitten by a snake or attacked by a wild animal was safer than being discovered by the mob above me.

With that thought in mind, I crawled through the sewer. When I could no longer hear voices outside, I began to calm down. The sewer seemed to go on forever, but I finally reached an opening at the other end. To my surprise, I was an entire block away from where I had entered.

I stood up, brushed as much filth off my clothes as I could and prepared to go home and confess to Mama what her darling children had been done. That's when Noah and Gabriel came running back, their shirts clinging to their wet bodies.

"What happened to you?" Noah asked apprehensively.

"Don't even try it," I snapped, madder than a bat out of hell. "You know what happened to me. You left me!"

I burst into tears.

Noah must have read my mind because he pleaded, "Don't tell Mama. Please."

I didn't say a word.

"We ran off, but we came back for you," he added.

"I'm going to tell Mama, so you can just stop your begging," I announced. "I could have been killed. You don't care about me. All you care about is your silly game."

"Ah, shucks," Gabriel replied, trying to sound convincing. "That man was just trying to scare you."

"You'll fall for anything," Noah added.

"I don't care how stupid you try to make me look. I'm still telling Mama and that's all I have to say!"

We walked home in silence. God must have been on our side, because when we got there, Mama was in the bathroom. I slipped into my room and changed into clean clothes. I knew I couldn't invent a believable excuse for looking the way I did. The easiest thing would have been to spill my guts, but I couldn't rat on my brothers. Besides, I would get myself into trouble if I told on them. I had been a willing participant, and Mama would punish me too. The family rule was if we wanted to tell on someone, we told because we wanted to help that person, not because we were angry. Telling after the fact would be breaking one of Mama's rules, so I would be better off to keep my mouth shut.

As I lay in bed, the events of the night brought muffled giggles. The whole thing had been pretty hilarious. That old prune-faced man had scared the mess out of me! I laughed when I though of how ridiculous I must have looked crawling through that sewer, crying for my mama. For a night that had started out so badly, things had turned out better than I had expected. Gabriel had been right. The man had only been trying to scare me. The incident made me take a candid look at myself. I had been having fun at someone else's expense. I had not cared how much damage I was doing to other people's property. I had been selfish. I had not even realized that what I was doing was wrong until I had felt threatened. Shame engulfed me. I knew I was a better person than I had demonstrated. I got on my knees and asked God to forgive my selfish, cruel acts. According to what Mama and Daddy had taught me, I was supposed to go to the people I had offended and ask their forgiveness, but I was afraid to do that. Instead, I vowed to volunteer to clean the church on Saturday evenings without grumbling or complaining. I would do it from my heart. I wondered whether Mama would see the difference in my attitude. I was certain that God would.

***

Love can kill. I know it's a fact, because I almost died from too much love last night. I made Mama angry yesterday. I guess I disappointed her more than anything. She gave me a responsibility, and I let her down. Mama sorted some lima beans and told me to let them soak for an hour. She made all the preparations. She even fixed the seasoning for me. She placed the bacon strips in three-fourths cup of water. All I had to do was set the pot on the stove and turn on the eye.

Mama had an appointment at the beauty parlor, and somebody had to have Daddy's dinner ready when he came home. Daddy didn't care where Mama went as long as she was ready to put his food on the table exactly at six o'clock. That was his reward for a hard day's work.

I had good intentions. I had wanted to make Mama proud

of me, but I let her down. As soon as she left, I went to my room and started reading <u>Gone With The Wind</u>. I had been reading a couple chapters a day. I was fascinated by the Ashley Wilkes character. How could Scarlett be so in love with such a weak man? Besides, he was already married! I was so carried away with the Ashley Wilkes and Scarlett O'Hara affair that I forgot all about the lima beans. Becoming thirsty, I went into the kitchen to get some tea (I don't drink water). That's when I remembered the lima beans. I hurriedly put them into the pot Mama had prepared, but the beans were just beginning to simmer when Mama came home. I prepared myself for the inevitable.

She slammed pots together and threw things around, and then decided it was too late for the beans to get cooked. She opened two cans of peas, cooked rice (we eat rice every day), and heated up the leftover cornbread and pot roast. I liked the make-do dinner better than the one Mama had planned, but she said Daddy had wanted lima beans and because of me, he wouldn't have them. She started to whip me but decided that I should go to bed immediately after dinner. No television. That way I would remember my responsibility the next time she told me to do something. I told her that I would not eat if I could not stay up and watch television. She told me to "suit myself." I left the table without eating.

I cried when Mama sent me to my room, not because I was hungry, but because I was angry. It wasn't fair for her to punish me because I forgot to cook some stupid lima beans. It's not as if I had deliberately disobeyed her. I simply forgot. I am a thirteen year-old child, not a machine.

Although I wasn't sleepy, I tried to go to sleep. I like to sleep through bad times, but no matter how hard I tried, I couldn't fall asleep. I tossed and turned as sounds from the nightly television shows spilled over into my room. Around seven o'clock, Grandmama came into the room. I pretended to be asleep. She tapped me on the shoulder. I turned over, pretending to yawn. She put her right hand to her lips mouthing "Sh-h-h-h" as she concealed something in her left hand behind her back.

She sat on the edge of the bed and planted a kiss on my forehead. I sat up. She pulled her left hand from behind her back.

"Look what Grandmama brought you," she whispered, handing me a plate covered with foil.

It was filled with peas, pot roast, rice and cornbread as she nervously watched the door.

"I couldn't bring you anything to drink," she added. "I was afraid I'd get caught."

I put the plate on the table and gave her a hug.

"I love you, Grandmama. More than anyone else in the whole world," I said.

She kissed me again on the forehead and slipped out of the room. I hurriedly ate my dinner and dozed off to sleep. I began to dream that I was cruising down Main Street in a red and white convertible, top down, wearing white shades and a mink coat. A big grin decorated my glowing face. I was deliriously happy.

Then, someone was shaking me awake. I sat straight up in bed and saw Noah standing there, holding a roast sandwich. I thanked him and told him I would eat it later. He insisted, "No, eat it now. I can't go to bed knowing you're hungry."

"I'm not hungry," I protested.

I couldn't tell him that Grandmama had already fed me. He seemed hurt, so I ate the sandwich. That seemed to make him happy. He left without another word.

I dozed off again only to be shaken awake again. This time it was Daddy. He was standing beside my bed with a self-approving grin on his face.

"Look what Daddy brought you," he said. I didn't say anything. I was afraid that if I opened my mouth I would throw up all over him. He handed the plate to me. I took it and placed it on the night stand.

"Aren't you going to eat?" He asked.

"I'm not hungry, Daddy," I protested

"Nonsense," Daddy said. "You've done enough pouting for one night. It's time to fill up that little stomach of yours. We can't have Daddy's favorite girl hungry, can we?"

"No, Sir." I answered.

I slowly unwrapped the plate.

Daddy continued, "I volunteered to wash the dishes so I could raid the refrigerator. I made you a peanut butter and jelly sandwich and a ham and cheese sandwich. I hope that will be enough."

I took a bite of the ham and cheese. With each chew the bread seemed to swell larger and larger. Satisfied that I was eating, Daddy left the room.

I forced myself out of bed and locked the door. I didn't want to take a chance on someone else bringing me food. My stomach was killing me. I will never again go to bed without supper. It would be hard to explain getting sick from overeating when I didn't eat!

***

Today was the first time I didn't get to attend the air show at Moody Air Force Base. Mama and I had a big blowout. Actually, it was a battle that I lost. I don't understand how things got so out of hand, but somehow we both lost control of our tempers.

Every year Moody Air Force Base sends buses to the different communities to transport anyone who wants to see the air show. Usually we prepare the night before, but this time we didn't. On a typical Saturday I sleep in late, but I arose early, hoping to be told that we would be attending the air show. I waited and waited. When I could no longer keep still, I marched into the kitchen and approached Mama.

Without stopping her work, she informed me that the air show had completely slipped her mind. She had said it in a matter-of-fact voice. Her tone indicated that was the end of the conversation, but I was determined to have my say. She turned back to the sink and resumed washing dishes. For some unknown reason, turning her back to me infuriated me.

Full of fury, I lashed out at Mama. "Tell me why we can't go to the air show."

She answered carefully, "To tell you the truth, I forgot all about it."

"It's not too late," I insisted.

"I've made other plans for the day. Ask your daddy. If he says you can go, you can go." She had spoken each word deliberately and softly, but I could still tell she was annoyed with me.

I stood before her silent for a few seconds. Then I pranced off, twisting my hips in a manner that announced I was a thirteen and should be treated like an adult. I twisted off looking for Daddy. I found him in the front yard trimming the hedges.

"Daddy, may we go to the air show?" I asked as I approached him.

"Ask your Mama," he said.

"She told me to ask you," I reported.

"Well, I'll go along with whatever she says."

I walked up to him and asked, "When are you going to be your own man?"

Daddy threw his clippers down and slapped at me. I ducked, leaving his hand to fan air.

"What's got into you?" Daddy asked. "You've never acted this way before."

"I'm just tired of you being henpecked." I burst into tears. "Why can't you be your own man?"

"Baby Girl, don't talk that way," Daddy pleaded.

"Why don't you stop petting her!" Mama said.

"Nobody's talking to you!" I snapped.

Before I could say another word, Mama had grabbed me and begun shaking me. In the scuffle, I lost my balance and fell in front of the refrigerator. Mama was reaching down toward me when Daddy pulled her back by the waist.

"That's enough, Candy," Daddy said in a low voice.

I could hear the hurt in her voice. I hadn't meant to hurt her. I wanted to apologize, but I decided to wait until Mama had had time to cool off. I had gone too far, and I knew it. I'll just stay out of her way until Daddy talks it over with her. Somehow he always makes everything all right.

***

I'll have to overcome my pride and admit I had a good time tonight. Mama and I had another one of our fights and, as usual, she won. I'm a teenager, but she still treats me like a child. She won't let anyone take me to a school banquet. How much trouble could I get into in a school cafeteria sitting around a table with parents and teachers chaperoning?

I met the most handsome boy Monday. He's six feet, three inches tall and looks like a bronze god. He is so cute! His eyes sparkled when he looked at me. Everyone is always telling me how smart I am, but no one ever tells me I'm pretty. He told me I looked like a little, chocolate doll. Then he asked me who was taking me to the band banquet. I lied and told him I hadn't made up my mind to go. He said if I decided to go, he would like to take me. Those words were music to my ears, but I knew they wouldn't make any difference in my life. Mama would never let him take me to the banquet. It would have to be Gabriel or nothing! All the other girls would have dates, but I would be escorted by one of my brothers.

In a way what happened tonight was my fault. I should have told Mama that I had given Donnell permission to escort me to the banquet. I didn't want him to know that I didn't date, but I was too afraid to ask Mama. What was the use? I knew she would only say no.

Around five o'clock I knew I had to do something, because Donnell was picking me up at seven, and I didn't want Mama to embarrass either of us. Daddy wasn't home, so that made my job even harder. He wouldn't have given me permission to go out with a boy, but he would have petted me when Mama broke my heart.

I decided the dinner table was the best place to make the announcement about my impending date. I would do it immediately after we said grace. Gabriel blessed the food, but I still said nothing. After Mama had passed the cabbage, roast beef, and cornbread she asked that old familiar question: "What did you do today?"

Without further prompting, we all knew to relate what had happened at school as vividly as we could down to the smallest detail. Gabriel volunteered first.

"Mrs. Lawson sent me to the principal's office."

"What for?" Mama asked, trying not to sound annoyed as she busied herself pouring tea for everyone.

"Nothing! Gabriel announced. She told all of us to line up, girls on one side of the room and boys on the other. Then she told the girls to march around so she could inspect their socks. When she finished, she told the boys to roll up their pants and come to her one by one. When she got to me I refused to roll my pants up. She got angry and sent me to the principal!"

"The nerve of that woman!" Mama exclaimed in disgust. "She's gone too far this time. I'm going to have *her* in the principal's office first thing tomorrow morning."

Mama was angry at the school! That was the perfect time to tell her about my date.

"Donnell's taking me to the band banquet tonight."

There! I had said it and hadn't been struck dead.

"What did you say?"

"Donnell's taking me to the band banquet tonight," I repeated.

All talking at the table ceased.

In a low but determined tone Mama said, "Donnell's not taking you anywhere." Who the hell is Donnell anyway?"

"He's the most gorgeous boy I've ever met."

I tried to say it with little or no emotion, hoping no one could hear my heart pounding with anticipation.

"Well, you had just better put Mr. Wonderful out of your mind. Wait until I tell your daddy about this!"

Becoming angry I said, "Daddy would probably let Donnell take me to the dance if it wasn't for you."

"That's enough," she snapped. "This discussion is closed."

"That what you always do," I interjected. "You close the discussion and don't give anyone else a chance to voice their opinion."

"I never said I was fair." she said with a sly grin. I didn't see anything amusing about her remark. Noah and Gabriel thought it was hilarious. They laughed wildly because they knew I couldn't stand being teased.

Noah started chanting, "Baby Girl's in love, Baby Girl's in love."

Gabriel joined him.

"You stop that"! I yelled. "Mama, tell them to stop!"

"That's enough! Everybody eat your dinner."

By this time tears were dripping involuntarily into my plate. In a defiant voice I said, "I don't want to eat. I want to go to the banquet with Donnell." I had surprised myself. I was getting braver and braver.

"Well, you're not going, young lady."

"Why? Give me one good reason why!"

"Because I said so," she replied, emphasizing the word I.

I continued to look down into my plate. I was actually trying to hide my tears.

"As long as you live in this house, you will go by my rules."

She looked me straight in the eyes and said, "We need to get our positions straight. I'm the mother. You're the daughter. I'm your father's wife. That makes me queen of the castle. Now, you can be the little princess, but if you want to be queen, you'll have to find your own castle. Is that clear?"

The words "Yes, Ma'am" rolled painfully off my tongue. Now, don't get me wrong. I love my mama, but when she makes those speeches I get the urge to run away from home. The only problem is I don't have anywhere to go. I'm just stuck. I can't wait until I'm grown.

Gabriel spoke up. "Oh, let 'er go. I'll go along to see that nothing happens. I hate to see her cry."

"I'll change my mind when she cries blood," Mama answered dryly.

That did it for me. I ran to my room, threw myself onto the bed, and yelled as loudly as I could. I wanted to upset Mama as much as she had upset me. I kicked and hollered, but she never said a word about it. When my throat began to hurt, I realized I was losing the battle. I stopped crying and started daydreaming about living in a California villa. I was miraculously transformed from a south Georgia chocolate girl into a West Coast beauty. Exotic, penetrating eyes enhanced my too-mysterious look as I strolled along the beach with my chiffon skirt rippling in the wind. Life in California was everything it was not in Georgia.

I don't know how long I had been lost in dreamland, but I did know I felt much better. I looked at the clock and saw it was already six. I ran to the door and called out to Gabriel.

"Get dressed," I said. "We have a banquet to attend."

***

Tonight was my shining hour. It was even better than when I was crowned Miss Pine Grove Junior High during the homecoming festivities. I delivered the first honor student's speech at our eighth grade graduation exercises. The subject was "The Night Brings Out the Stars." I didn't understand the part about the night being a more familiar friend to me than man, but I didn't tell Mrs. S. She says I'm precocious and should go far in life. I asked her what precocious meant, and she said that means I know more than I should at my age. I figure she knows what she's talking about, because I do my brother's homework. He's four grades ahead of me.

Anyway, I was really good tonight. Everybody said so. Mama and Daddy were smiling proudly. I know I'll forget most of the speech, but I wrote down my special part: "It is the dark hours of life that teach us to discriminate between the true and false, the fair-weathered friends, and the faithful comrades."

I'll have to remember that when I'm filthy rich, famous, and living in California.

***

Daddy preached his trial sermon today. Mama didn't go to church with us, so I had to be her stand-in. I didn't like being the center of attention, but I was happy to be able to help my daddy. He has wanted to be a minister since he was a little boy.

The deacons wanted to know where Mama was. Daddy told everybody Mama was sick. She really wasn't. Daddy had been drinking the night before, and she said he ought not play with God that way. Daddy had argued that there was nothing wrong with taking a little nip as long as you didn't hurt anyone. Mama still refused because she said she didn't want to see Daddy preach his own damnation. I could never picture Daddy in hell because he is a good man.

I knew Daddy was going to be all right from the moment he outlined his hymn.

"Father, I stretch my hands to thee, no other help I know. If thou withdrew thyself from me, o wither shall I go."

The words dripped like honey from his lips.

When I looked at the congregation, smiling old ladies were fanning and moving their heads from left to right. A few raised their fans toward heaven and shouted, "Yes, Lord! Hallelujah!"

My mind wandered to the food that would be spread out on the table under the shade trees. I could pick what I wanted to eat, and I was going to eat lots of chocolate cake!

By the time Daddy gave his text, he had the congregation eating out of his hands.

"I am He," he shouted, strutting across the pulpit like a proud rooster.

When he got to the part about being Alpha and Omega, an old woman began to shout. She raised both hands into the air and spun around repeatedly. On one of her spins, her wig flew off. She stopped shouting, stooped down, picked up her wig, and quietly sat back down. She did not raise her head again until Daddy's sermon was over.

At the end of the sermon everybody congratulated Daddy and me. I didn't see that I had done anything of significance, but Daddy said I had saved the day for him. I felt a little guilty, because I had winked at several boys while I pretended to be wrapped up in Daddy's sermon. If you ask me, Mama should have been sitting in the chair facing the altar. She was the one who vowed to God to love, honor, cherish, and obey Daddy— not me. I'm just a child. Besides, I wouldn't marry a preacher, anyway. Preacher's wives can't smoke or drink. If I'm going to live in California, I'll have to throw champagne parties and smoke cigarettes in long, fancy holders like the ladies do in the movies.

***

I will never steal another one of Daddy's hot sodas as long as I live. I feel like someone is pounding my head with a hammer. Mama says I have a hangover. She's mad at me, but it's not my fault. It's Daddy's fault. He's the one who put the liquor in the Pepsi bottle. I only drank it. Daddy had a soda hidden in the corner of the bedroom behind my trunk. I saw the soda. I am used to drinking hot sodas, but that one burned every inch it traveled down my throat. After drinking the soda, I got so sleepy.

Everybody in the house has a favorite show. Grandmama's

is "Lawrence Welk"; Gabriel and Noah, "Rawhide"; Mama, "The Ed Sullivan Show"; Daddy, "Have Gun Will Travel"; mine, "Wagon Train". I didn't want to miss it, so I told Gabriel to call me when the show came on.

I don't remember what happened, but Mama said she reminded Gabriel to tell me that "Wagon Train" was on. Gabriel said he called out to me, but I didn't answer. He came to the bed and shook me.

"Baby Girl," he said, "Come on," Wagon Train" is on."

Gabriel knew that I wouldn't miss "Wagon Train" for anything in the world. Knowing I would be angry about missing the show, he shook me harder.

"Leave me alone," I finally answered lethargically.

"'Wagon Train' is on," he said.

According to Gabriel I said, "Damn 'Wagon Train'."

Gasping in disbelief, Gabriel ran to the living room shouting, "Mama, there's something wrong with Baby Girl. She's talking like a drunk person. She's cursing!"

"Hush lying," Mama said.

She came into the room to see what was wrong with me.

"Baby Girl, wake up. "Wagon Train" is on."

To Mama's disbelief, I sat straight up in the bed and said, "Call me the damn 'Wagon Train'."

Gabriel said that's when Mama lost her cool. She grabbed me and tried to shake the daylights out of me. My body moved back and forth like a rag doll.

"You must be crazy or something," Mama said.

By this time Daddy, Grandmama, Gabriel, and Noah were all in the room. Knowing the signs of being tipsy, Daddy went into the front bedroom and brought the empty Pepsi bottle back with him. Although he knew he was going to have a fight with Mama, he told her he had put some bourbon in a

Pepsi and had hidden it behind my trunk. He had made several trips to the bedroom when Mama hadn't been looking. When he went back for another sip, he had found the bottle empty. Mama didn't whip me. She said the hangover was punishment enough. Boy was she right! I would feel better if I could take my head off and set it on the dresser until the alcohol gets out of my system. Until then, I'll just stay in my room and pray Mama and Daddy forgive me for being so stupid.

***

If I didn't know any better, I'd say someone has roots on me. But believing in roots is believing in Satanism.

Miss Lawson, Cousin Mark, and I went to pick blueberries. We were to get paid forty cents a quart. I planned to pick twelve quarts. That way I could buy the patent leather shoes I saw at Butler's. The shoes were three dollars and ninety-eight cents plus tax. Who knows? I might even pick fifteen quarts.

When we reached the blueberry farm, I was disappointed. I had expected to find rows of bushes loaded with blueberries. Instead I saw rows and rows of trees five and six feet tall stretching for miles. I didn't see how I was going to pick the berries. I was too short.

Miss Lawson took us to a shed and gave us ladders. I'm afraid of heights, but I didn't want anyone to know it. I had to figure out a way to pick the berries and still feel safe while on the ladder. A light went on in my head. Instead of holding the bucket, I tied it around my waist. That way both of my hands were free. I hurried from tree to tree picking blue berries. Before I knew it, I had two quarts! I was eighty cents closer to purchasing my shoes. I was so happy! Then it happened.

My head started to hurt. I kept on picking blueberries. I was not going to let a little thing like a headache stop me. I carefully descended the ladder and started moving it to another tree. A pain hit me in the pit of my stomach. It drew me double. I had never hurt that badly before. The pain let up a little. I attempted to move the ladder closer to the next tree. Another pain hit me followed by another and another. Then I had the urgent need to use the bathroom. There was no outdoor toilet, so I found a large bush to squat behind. Lucky for me, I had a pack of Kleenex in my pocket. That's when I noticed the blood. I realized I was having my first period. I had heard girls talk about it at school. They thought it was wonderful, but I didn't see anything so great about the pain. I had also heard my brothers joking with their friends about girls "being on the rag". I didn't want them to find out about me, because it hurts me to be teased.

As I worried about hiding my womanhood, I started gagging. Miss Lawson said she had better take me home. She had a look of disgust on her face as she reluctantly agreed to give up picking berries. The ride home was pure hell. I thought she looked for every bump in the road to hit as hard as she could. Each bump sent piercing pains through my body. By the time we reached home, I had vomited all over my clothes. I went inside, changed clothes, took a BC, and went to bed. I left a note for Mama on the kitchen table.

Grandmama got home first. She saw the note and, without putting down her handbag, she came into the room and sat on the side of my bed. She put her hand on my head.

"You're hot," she said. "How do you feel?"

"I hurt so badly, Grandmama." I said.

"Show Grandmama where the pain is."

I placed her hand on my stomach. "The pain starts here and travels upward. The higher the pain travels the less it hurts."

"Did you fall?"

"No, I said somewhat embarrassed. "I started my period today."

"Oh," she said. "Now that we know what the problem is, we can do something about it."

She patted my hand reassuredly and said, "I'll be right back. Grandmama is going to fix everything."

She was gone for only a few minutes. She returned carrying a tray. On the tray were a sugar container, spoon, orange soda, and a bottle of turpentine. She had a big towel draped over her arm.

"When Candy gets her, we'll go and buy a belt and sanitary napkins for you. Meanwhile, fold this towel and lie on it."

"The first day is always light. You're in pain because the blood is not flowing freely."

She put the tray on the night stand and ordered me to sit up.

"I have something for you to take. It's nasty, but it'll make you feel better."

"What is it?" I asked.

She didn't say a word. She filled the tablespoon with sugar, dropped nine drops of turpentine on the sugar, then held the spoon in my direction.

"Here take this," she commanded. I knew better than to argue with her. I took the spoon in my right hand. She placed the soda in my left hand.

"Drink it," she insisted.

I emptied the contents of the spoon and swallowed quickly.

"Yuk!" I exclaimed as the turpentine made me want to throw up. I tried to drown the taste with the soda, but the turpentine overpowered it. I knew I was in for a long day.

Then Grandmama did something peculiar. She turned the turpentine bottle upside down and shook it vigorously. Then she made an X on my stomach with her index finger.

"Now," she said, "the pain will go away."

I didn't know how Grandmama knew, but just like she said, the pain went away. Soon I was asleep, dreaming about riding the waves on a California beach.

My dream took me far away from sandy spurs, blueberry fields, and racism to a land of opportunity and fun.

***

All my life I've wanted to work during the summer, but the only jobs available to teenagers are picking cotton and working in tobacco fields. Mama doesn't do field work, so I have to stay home with her. Noah and Gabriel, like most of my classmates, get to work every summer. Mama says it's all right for them to do field work because they're boys. I don't see what being a girl has to do with making money. I like to spend money just as much as Noah and Gabriel do. I wanted to be able to go downtown and spend money that I have earned myself. It's a matter of pride.

This summer I finally got my long, awaited chance. A man named Gus hired Noah to assemble a crew to top the tobacco in his field. Noah asked Mama's permission for me to go. He promised to see that no physical harm came to me, and he promised that he would not let any boys near me. Noah's promise was not news to me, because he always squealed on me whenever I was sweet on a boy. After some fast talking, Mama agreed to let me work for a day. She was convinced that after working one day I would never want to see another tobacco field. She told me that I could keep whatever money I made if I bought something to wear to school. That offer appealed to me because I had seen a pair of black patent leather shoes in Butler's window that I wanted. A four-dollar price tag advertised they were in my price range. I wondered how much I would make in the tobacco field.

Friday night I went to bed without being told, eager to arise the next morning full of energy. I tossed and turned most of the night as I listened to night sounds. When I did doze off, I dreamed of shoes. I was sitting on a red velvet couch in Butler's Shoe Store being brought shoes to try on by a young, handsome salesman. Shoes of different colors were all around me—red, blue, green, aqua, yellow, purple, brown, black, gray, silver, and gold. Shoes were everywhere, and the most wonderful part of the whole thing was that I could choose as many pairs as I wanted. I was about to try on a pair of black patent leather shoes when Mama's voice interrupted.

"Time to get up."

We got out of bed, dressed, and forced down a hearty breakfast. I did not want to eat at five a.m., but Mama insisted that we needed strength in order to work in the field. She said we would sweat and the loss of body fluids would drain our energy. As we passed by her going out the door, she handed each of us a sack lunch. When Noah reached her, she gave him a plastic bottle filled with water she had frozen overnight. She said the ice would melt gradually, and we would have cool water to drink most of the day. Mama had left no stone unturned. She gave me a scarf to shield my face from the sun and one of her discarded Sunday-go-to-meeting hats to protect my head. She told me to put green leaves in the hat's crown. The leaves would keep the sun's rays from beaming directly on the mole of my head. Mama said it was to protect us from heat stroke, but I suspect it was to protect us from brain damage. Our family is known for being intellectuals. Surely we wouldn't want to do anything that would jeopardize our status symbol.

In the midst of her warnings, a loud beep beckoned us for work. We climbed aboard a large truck, I with some difficulty, and huddled together to protect ourselves from the raw morning air as the old truck rattled toward our destination.

About thirty minutes later, we reached a field in Morven, Georgia. Mr. Gus sat on the hood of his truck and gave us instructions for the day. The first thing he told us he wanted us to do was to break the blossoms out of the top of the tobacco stalks. That sounded simple enough, but when he told us to remove all the suckers from the plants, I gave Noah a confused look. I had no idea what Mr. Gus was talking about. The only suckers I had ever heard my brothers talk about were a stick of candy and a person who let someone else make a fool of him. Noah whispered to me that he would show me what to do. According to Gus, it was so simple that even a moron could do it.

Mr. Gus got in his truck, cranked up, and drove a little piece down the road. Then he backed up.

"I have an idea," he said as he came around the truck to where we were standing. "Since today is Saturday, I know you all want to get home and get some shopping done."

He had my attention.

"I was going to pay you ten dollars for a day's work..."

My mind quickly calculated, "I can afford two pairs of shoes."

"So," he continued. "If you finish by noon, I'll still pay you for a full day."

Sounds of agreement came from the group.

"Just don't do a sloppy job. I'll see you at noon."

Noah called us together and gave us a pep talk. He inspired us to finish the tobacco field by noon. I didn't need much encouragement, because I wanted to get to Butler's before it closed. Noah told everyone to select a row. He put me on a row between Gabriel and him. That way he said they could keep me up with everyone else. He showed me how to top the tobacco. That was easy because all I was doing was breaking some flowers from the stalk's top. Removing the suckers was a different story. Many of the suckers were as large as the leaves. Noah said Gus had been cheap. He should have had the tobacco suckered weeks ago. Nevertheless, he told us to do our best because we had made a deal.

We ran into the field eager to start the day. We reasoned that the sooner we started, the sooner we would finish. We worked with a steady rhythm—up one row and down another, up one row and down another. The rounds seemed endless. In my tiredness, I sometimes mistakenly tore off tobacco instead of suckers. Whenever that happened, I hid the tobacco leaves under weeds. I would rest long enough to remember what Noah had taught me about recognizing suckers. Then I would take off down the row, removing tops and suckers as fast as I could. To save time we agreed to skip lunch so we could finish early.

We did our best to finish by noon, but we didn't make it. Noah told us to keep working. He counted the number of rows we had left and decided that we could finish by one o'clock if each person carried two rows. I had trouble keeping up one row, but Noah looked at me and said, "Don't worry. Gabriel and I will keep you up."

I don't know how Noah did it, but he hit the nail right on the head. At one o'clock sharp we walked out of the field. We had finished every row. As we neared the edge of the field, we could see Mr. Gus's truck. We cheered and raced toward the truck. The look that Mr. Gus gave us is seared into my memory. My first thought was he knew about the tobacco I had accidentally destroyed, but I realized he had no way of knowing that. It had to be something else. His eyes followed us carefully as we splashed our faces with water, washed our hands, and exchanged congratulations. We were going home soon and with a day's pay. While all this was going on, Mr. Gus silently stood by. Noah told us to get in line to receive our pay. Since he had put the crew together, he moved to the front of the line. Mr. Gus reached into the cab of the truck and retrieved his money pouch. Then he came around the side of his truck to where we were standing

We were disappointed. We wanted him to say something about the good job we had done, but he said nothing. Instead, he seemed annoyed that we had been dependable workers. Mama and Daddy have always taught us that any job worth doing is worth doing well. We don't know any other way to be.

"Come on and get your pay!" he called out.

My heart did a pitter-patter at the sound of the word money.

Noah held his hand out. When he didn't put the money in his pocket and move out of Gabriel's way, I knew something was wrong.

"What is this?" Noah asked.

"That's your pay," Mr. Gus answered.

"This is only five dollars," Noah said. "You owe me five more."

"I don't owe you nothin', boy!" Mr. Gus screamed furiously.

His anger magnified every wrinkle on his face.

"You promised to pay us ten dollars to top and sucker your field!" Noah argued as resentment began to show on his face.

"You haven't done a day's work!" Mr. Gus insisted. It's only one o'clock. "You don't expect me to just give my money away, do you?"

Noah took several steps toward Mr. Gus and said in a low, demanding tone, "I want what's due me."

Mr. Gus backed up toward the truck's front door, his eyes settling on the shotgun hung on the rack in the cab of his truck. Not knowing what was about to happen next, I jumped in between Mr. Gus and Noah.

"Let it go, Noah," I said. "It's all right if we don't get paid what Mr. Gus promised. We're away from home and we don't have an adult with us."

"I'm not worried about myself," Noah assured me. "I've let you all down."

"No, you haven't."

"We don't blame you."

"Take the five dollars, man."

"Yeah, let's get out of here."

Noah looked deeply into Mr. Gus' eyes and said, "Thank you." The sarcasm in Noah's voice echoed throughout the field..

One by one we accepted our pay and refused to look at the man who had cheated us.

Cheating us had not been enough for Mr. Gus. Instead of taking us back to our neighborhood where he had picked us up, he made us unload downtown near the railroad tracks where colored people hang out on Saturdays. Weary and tired, we walked home. We passed by some of our schoolmates, but I was not as ashamed as I though I would be. As a matter of fact, I was proud of myself. I had done a day's work, and I had kept peace in a situation that could have been explosive. People's lives are more important than money anyway. So what if I'll be able to buy only one pair of shoes?   A person can wear only one pair of shoes at a time anyway.

***

We went to see that ugly old woman in Douglas again. Mama said she had had a hysterectomy. I asked Mama what that was. She said that's when a woman has all her female organs taken out. She's been spaded like a dog. Family members whispered that that was the reason why her husband left her for a younger woman. She can't have any children. I personally don't see that as a loss to society, but Mama said that a man doesn't want to start constructing a building knowing he will never have a chance to finish it. There should be something to show for hard work. Personally, I consider her infertility as a blessing. The world doesn't need another person as ugly as she is.

***

Christmas is always my favorite time of the year, but this Christmas was extra special. I received the best present I have ever been given. To my surprise, it was a gift selected and paid for by Gabriel. That's what made it priceless.

Around six o'clock Gabriel called home. He told me that he would miss our usual Christmas Eve festivities because he had to work until midnight, but he wanted me to stay up until he came home. He had a special present that was too good to keep until morning.

As customary, we gathered in the living room around the tree to exchange gifts. This was our first aluminum tree. There was a revolving light that changed the tree's colors red, blue, green, and silver. I thought it was beautiful, but Daddy didn't like artificial trees. He liked the smell of pinecones. We sang

"Silent Night." Then Daddy thanked God for letting us be alive to celebrate another Christmas Eve. He also added thanks for having reasonable health, wealth, jobs, loved ones, etc. Mama cleared her throat. That was her signal for Daddy to cut the prayer short. That's when I thanked God. I wanted to open my present, but Daddy wouldn't let us touch the presents until we sang "O Little Town of Bethlehem".

As the words "Are met in thee tonight" poured from our lips, we raced for the tree, searching for our names. I found Matthew's gift first. His little fingers tore excitedly at the paper until he unwrapped a teddy bear.

"Open yours first," I urged Mama.

Mama eagerly ripped the paper from her gift. We had bought her a salad bowl with wood tongs. It was something that she had always wanted but had never taken the time or money to buy.

Daddy opened his gift next. I had selected it. He had a bottle of Old Spice. He opened it and splashed a little on his face. Then he grabbed me and gave me an "I love you" hug. He knew that present had come from me. It's what I give him every year!

Noah opened his gift next. He had six pairs of socks of different colors. He gave a dull but polite "thank you."

Then I opened my big mouth and said, "Why don't we open Gabriel's gift?"

Daddy said, "Since it was your idea, you open the gift."

I unwrapped the neatly folded package and placed Gabriel's gift on the coffee table. He too had received socks for a gift. Noah rushed over and began to count: one, two, three, four, five, six, seven, eight. I couldn't imagine why he was counting. "Who bought Gabriel these socks?"

"I did," Grandmama answered. "Why?"

"Why did he get eight pairs when I only got six?"

Grandmama said, "I got the two extra pairs for the price of one. They just happened to be Gabriel's size."

"Uh huh," Noah said. Then he shot Grandmama a threatening look and pointed his finger at her. "I'm going to fix you," he said. "Just you wait and see."

The way he said it was funny, so we all laughed. We couldn't believe his petty jealousy. He was eighteen years old and still acting like a spoiled brat!

"Boy, you're getting too big for your britches," Daddy warned. "I'm going to have to take you down a notch or two to help you remember you're still a child."

Noah gave Daddy one of those looks that said, "No, I'm not."

"You're still a child," Daddy repeated. "You may be a foot taller than I am, but you're still a child, and you will be respectful to everyone as long as you live in this house."

Noah started to walk away. Daddy said, "Come back here."

Grandmama touched Daddy on the arm and said, "Oh, let the boy go. He'll be alright in the morning."

That little incident seemed to have put a damper on the evening. There appeared to be a chill in the air that I had not noticed before.

Grandmama, Mama, and Cousin Ruth continued preparing for Christmas Day. Mama took the first cake from the china cabinet and moistened it with wine before setting it on the buffet next to a chocolate cake—my favorite. Daddy's favorite, a coconut cake, was next to mine. Mama cut a slice of her favorite, a pound cake, and left it on the table for Santa Claus. Matthew wanted to be sure Santa got a slice. She put the creamer and sugar dish next to an empty cup and saucer.

She left the coffee pot on so he could have hot coffee. I always wondered who actually ate the cake.

Daddy, Mama, Grandmama, and Cousin Ruth finally went to bed. I stayed up waiting for Gabriel. I turned off the lights and watched the tree change colors. The revolving color wheel lulled me to sleep.

I don't know when Gabriel got home, but I heard him calling my name and shaking me. There was a beautifully wrapped package on the coffee table. It was really too pretty to open.

"Open it," Gabriel urged.

I carefully removed the red velvet bow from the package, because I wanted to keep it. Gabriel was more excited than I was. He took the top off and handed me the small package. It contained a pair of size eight and a half stockings.

"I didn't know what color to buy so I got you red fox. That's what color Mama wears."

I didn't care what color they were. They were real stockings—the kind grownups wear. Gabriel had thought of everything. He even had a pair of garters for me.

"I knew you'd need something to hold them up," he announced proudly. "Now, for the grand finale," he said as he gestured in the manner of a ring master. He took the lid off a box that contained a pair of heels. They were breathtaking. The shoes were red, accented with a black toe and heel. I slipped them on and stumbled around the living room. I would have to practice, but I could learn to walk like a lady.

Last night marked the beginning of my passage from childhood to womanhood. I will always cherish Gabriel for recognizing that I was changing, and this change needed to be reflected on the outside. I'm sure I'll receive many more gifts in my lifetime, some more expensive, but nothing will be more precious to me than my black and red patent leather heels.

CHAPTER 6
MAJOR CHANGE—1957

Daddy came home very angry today. Yesterday he was told he would be getting a new boss. When his new boss showed up today, Daddy said his eyes almost popped from his head. It was the boy he had trained for two weeks! Daddy had taught him how to pull and saw lumber according to the grade. Last week he had called Daddy Mr. Moore. Now Daddy was told he had to call the boy Mr. Wright. Daddy said he can't be any more than twenty years old. If it weren't for his family, Daddy said he would quit his job. But he has to keep food on the table and a roof over our heads.

There's no union at the lumberyard, so the boss can do whatever he wants. If Daddy complains, he will just be fired. Daddy says he doesn't know how long he will be able to keep letting someone use him and put him down. He's afraid one day someone is going to say the wrong thing to him and he's going to explode.

***

We sat around the heater tonight putting puzzles together. Mama says it's good exercise for the mind. There had been an article in the <u>Daily Times</u> about the buses being integrated in Montgomery, Alabama. The article sparked a lively conversation during our family time. Daddy voiced his anger at a white lady who had said in a TV interview that she didn't understand what the colored people wanted. Daddy said we wanted what everyone else wanted—a decent living.

With that comment, Daddy did what he loved to do best. He drifted into telling stories about the past. He said that during slavery, milk was poured into troughs and little children drank from them like animals. Even when he was growing up, according to Daddy, his mother would help the quarter master kill hogs. He would give her the hog's head and internal organs. I guess that's why Daddy likes hog brains and chitterlings so much! In a bowl, Mama mixes the brains with eggs. Daddy likes them lightly scrambled. He also likes trite, hog maw, and mountain oysters. Daddy said the name "mountain oysters" makes eating a hog's testicles sound like a delicacy. He had no trouble satisfying his appetite, because Mama didn't eat hog's brains or mountain oysters, and neither did we children.

After Daddy finished telling about eating hog guts, Mama told us about her father's life before she was born. She admiringly referred to her daddy as Papa. Now she didn't like his wayward ways, but she liked the way he stood up to white folks. She said her daddy's father had worked as a sharecropper. He rented from his boss and charged all his clothes, food, and supplies to the mill store. At the end of the season, her granddaddy would go to the office to receive his check. When all his yearly rent, fertilizer, and clothes charges were added up, the boss would tell him, "You almost got out of debt this year. I'll add what you still owe me to next year's bill."

Her grandfather had worked an entire year and had not even made a penny profit. He had told his wife that he had had enough of farming. It was killing him. He couldn't even take his family shopping in town. That night he had packed the little belongings they had on his wagon and slipped away. There would be no next year for him.

Daddy said things haven't changed that much. Colored people still work for slave wages.

Mama's great-grandmother's life hadn't been any better. In addition to the poverty, she had been brought up in an abusive home. Her daddy's word was gospel, even if he was wrong. His wife had been afraid of him. Therefore, she never disagreed with him for fear he would turn his wrath on her. One day Mama's grandfather announced to Grandmama that he had hired her out to work on a neighboring farm. She was just fourteen years old. An excellent student, she was already teaching elementary students. Her dream was to become an elementary school teacher. She could spell every word in her Webster Blue Back Speller. She wanted to teach students, not clean houses.

Grandmama said she became livid, and for the first time, she had talked back to her daddy. She hadn't meant to. The words just poured effortlessly from her mouth. Her father had called it sassing, but she had only been speaking from the heart. She had tried to explain how she thirsted for knowledge, how she longed to teach, but her words had fallen upon deaf ears. Her father had stood before her like the god he imagined himself to be and simply ignored her appeals. It had been as though they were on two separate planets, each one needing different nourishment in order to survive.

This time she would not give in. She was almost grown. Little buds stuck out in her bosom, a signal that a full bosom would soon follow. She had even been having her period for a year. According to nature, she was now a woman even if her father still saw her as an underling, incapable of making grownup decisions. When she had kept adamantly refusing to change her mind, he had slapped her and reminded her he was the head of the household. She didn't cry. She reminded herself that she could hold back the tears a few more hours. Then when everyone was asleep, she would slip away and never return. She loved her mother and brothers, but she was willing to give them up if it would mean a chance to be happy.

Before daybreak she had dressed, packed a pasteboard suitcase, and sneaked away from home. At first she walked stealthily, careful not to awake anyone. The further she traveled away from home, the braver she became. Her inner spirit affected her body language. Her steps became more rapid, her body straightened, and her chin seemed to reach for the sky. Her new freedom gave every step a sense of urgency as she hurried to her new fate.

Six months later she had a job in Fitzgerald working as a cook. She had met Papa and married him. They stayed together until he died.

***

Noah has graduated from high school. Mama and Daddy were excited, but Noah seemed to be bothered by the whole affair. I don't know whether or not anyone else noticed his behavior, but he appeared to be too preoccupied to take part in the family's celebration. He first started acting strangely last Sunday before the baccalaureate service. Mama asked him to go outside and pose for some photographs in his cap and gown. You would have thought someone had spat in his face. He finally gave in and posed in the yard beside the car. The picture turned out nice, but the frown on his face showed his resentment. I think he was trying to get away to see his girlfriend. I know love is important, but he will only graduate from high school once in a lifetime. As smart as he is, you'd think he would know this.

He has really shown no interest in graduation. He keeps

everything to himself, so I'll never know for sure what's bugging him. It could be so many things. He had problems at school about being selected valedictorian. We would have never known this if one of his teachers hadn't told Mama. According to the teacher, Noah and another student were given a chemistry test to determine who would receive the higher average. Noah had made the higher grade. The teachers decided to test them a second time. Noah made the higher score on that test too. Someone else suggested testing them a third time. That's when the teacher spoke up. She accused the faculty of trying to give an honor to their friend's son who had not earned it—-second place maybe, but not first.

Noah was awarded the honor of being valedictorian of his class, but he still had to face disappointment. All he had ever talked about was attending Morehouse College in Atlanta, Georgia. Noah received a scholarship, but it was to Tuskegee Institute in Alabama. He knows that Tuskegee is an excellent school, but attending Morehouse has always been his dream. Mama told Noah that we don't always get what we want, but we have to be thankful for what we get and make the most of it. She said sometimes our blessings come in disguises. To cheer him up, Mama and Daddy promised to take him to Tuskegee to visit the campus. If he didn't like it, they would help him go to Morehouse.

Mama, Daddy, and I went with Noah to Tuskegee. Grandmama stayed home with Gabriel and Matthew. I wanted to go because I'd read about George Washington Carver and Booker T. Washington. Imagine actually seeing where they had lived and worked. We took Noah to the freshman barracks to let him see where and how he would be living. Then we toured the campus. I will never forget the first time I looked up and saw the statue of Booker T. Washington raising the veil from the eyes of an unlearned man. The inscription was inspiring! I tore a piece of paper from a brown bag that we'd brought our lunch in and copied the inscription, which I would memorize on the ride home:

"The masses of us shall live by the production of our hands,
and we shall
prosper in proportion as we learn to dignify common labor
and put brains
and skills into the common occupation of life. There is no
defense or security
for any of us, except in the highest intelligence and
development of all of us."

I liked that quote because that's what Mama had always preached to us. She said that education was the only way that we as a people would be able to move forward.

After we left the statue, we visited the house where Mr. Washington had actually lived. His hat was still hanging in the room. From the house we went to the George Washington Carver Museum. His work was truly amazing. I had read about his accomplishments, but what I had visualized did not come close to describing his accomplishments. I would have never guessed that face powder had come from peanuts, and I never would have believed anyone who told me a colored man had invented it! I didn't know how Noah felt, but I liked that Tuskegee. For the first time in my life I was proud that I was colored. I had had the opportunity to see firsthand things I had only read about in books, and those accounts had done neither Mr. Washington nor Mr. Carver justice. I now knew what it felt like to be in the midst of greatness.

***

Gabriel has become quite the trumpeter. I really think he should go to the Juliard School of Music like Mr. Miller suggested. Gabriel doesn't want to go because he said he's had about as much of school as he can stand. He wants to form a band and travel around the country. Red and Daniel want to join him. They have been practicing together for over a year now.

Gabriel was hired to play at a club. Mama says he's too young to be out all hours of the night, but Grandmama and Daddy disagree. Grandmama says playing the trumpet is about the only thing Gabriel enjoys doing. Daddy said he would pick Gabriel up every night. Mama said she knew how long that would last. She finally gave in, but she said she knew she was going to end up being the one to pick him up every night.

Gabriel promised Mama that he would not do anything wrong. He said at night he hears himself playing like the angel Gabriel. Music was in his blood, he declared. All he wanted to do was to make beautiful music for people to dance to and music to inspire people to fall in love.

It wasn't about staying out late. It was just about one thing—making music.

**

When I turned to the sports section today, my eyeballs almost popped out of their sockets. There was a colored woman holding a tennis racket and flashing a victorious smile. She was identified as Althea Gibson. According to the article, she was the first colored woman to win the Women's Singles Championship at Wimbledon, England.

I cut the article out and pasted it in my scrapbook. I didn't know colored people even played tennis. I've never seen a real tennis court. We don't even have a community swimming pool.

I've always wanted to learn to swim, but I suppose I'll have to wait until I move to California. I tried swimming once when I went to the beach in Florida, but the waves kept knocking me down. Now tennis is something I could learn to play. I know I can hit a tennis ball, and I'm swift on my feet. Mama can make my outfit, but how will I get the money to buy my tennis racket?

***

Today was special. Grandmama and I fed Jesus. We didn't actually feed *Jesus*, but Grandmama said he could have been. We will never know. We were sitting on the back porch crocheting (Grandmama is teaching me how to crochet a stole) when a white man came up and asked for some work to do. He said he was hungry. Grandmama told him she didn't have any money, but she would give him some food. She told me to go into the kitchen and heat up the leftovers from breakfast. She stayed outside with the drifter.

I heated up several flapjacks and bacon and covered the flapjacks with maple syrup. I placed a hunk of butter on the flapjacks, went outside, and handed the plate and napkin to the drifter. He didn't use the fork on his plate. Instead, he broke the flapjacks with his fingers and started packing the food into his mouth. Then he licked each finger slowly and deliberately. Mama would have killed me if I had licked my fingers! Didn't he know why I had given him a napkin?

Grandmama sent me inside to get him something to drink. We were out of sodas, so I made him some sweet water. He asked Grandmama if he could take a nap. She told him he couldn't come inside, but he was welcome to nap on the porch. Grandmama and I went inside, locked the screen door, and continued our crocheting.

I asked Grandmama why she had fed a white man. I reminded her that he could be a member of the Ku Klux Klan. She said that could be true, but she was doing what Jesus would have done. When I asked her what she meant, she told me to put down my crocheting and get the Bible. She instructed me to find Proverbs 25:21 and read it aloud.

"If thine enemy be hungry, give him bread to eat
And if he be thirsty, give him water to drink;
For thou shalt heap coals of fire upon his head
And the Lord shall reward thee."

I told Grandmama I still thought is was dumb to be nice to someone who would probably kill us the first chance he got. Grandmama never gets angry, but I could tell she was becoming annoyed with me. She explained that regardless of what color we were, we were all God's children. She said the Bible commands us to "Love thy neighbor as thyself". Then she said something that made a lot of sense to me. She said God loves all of us, and every time we do something to help someone else, God smiles. According to Grandmama, that's what a rainbow is—a big smile from God to all his children of different colors.

"Do you know who that man is?" She asked.

I shook my head to answer no.

"That's right. You don't know who he is. Come here," she said in a stern voice. She flipped frantically through the Bible, handed it to me, pointed to a verse and said, "Read."

I read:

"Be not forgetful to entertain strangers; for thereby
some have entertained angels unawares."
Hebrews 13:2

I ran to the door, hoping to get a look at a real angel. The stranger had left.

***

"Ye thou I walk through the valley of the shadow of death, I will fear no evil, for thou art with me." Psalms 23:4

I attended Grandmama's wake tonight. It was a joyous occasion, just the way she would have wanted it to be. She always said we should cry when a baby is born into a world of trouble and rejoice when a person dies and goes to be with his heavenly Father. So it was no surprise that her wake became a night of celebration instead of a night of mourning. In the midst of eating fried chicken, potato salad, collard greens, cornbread, and sweet potato pie (the list of food that friends and relatives brought over could go on and on), everyone talked about Grandmama and how she had inspired them to live a life of humility and love.

As the night grew on, the celebration became more boisterous. I felt that some of the family members were making a mockery of Grandmama's wake. All the family members are Baptist and all good Baptists know, without being told, that drinking whiskey is a sin. So what does a good Christian Baptist do? He hides his bottle and makes secret trips to get a shot. Since Grandmama had never tasted a drop of liquor in her life (she swore on the Bible), I saw the drinking as being disrespectful to her.

Pains stabbed through my heart every time I saw someone march into the kitchen and return glassy-eyed, whispering to one another, "Boy, that was a good one."

As the trips became more frequent, the stories got funnier and funnier. Somehow I managed to get caught up in the excitement too. When Uncle Jimmy (my favorite uncle) told a story about Daddy before he, to quote Uncle Jimmy, "became a man of the cloth," I laughed so hard until I got a cramp in my side.

According to Uncle Jimmy, Daddy would go out every Saturday night to Cousin Ronnie's club. The café was located on South Patterson Street just below the railroad tracks. It was a few doors down from the Hole in the Wall. The Hole in the Wall was known as a "juke joint", but Cousin Ronnie's club was a place where respectable people could go and have a good time. At least that's what Daddy had told Mama. Actually, teenagers frequented the cafe by day, but it was rumored that Cousin Ronnie bootlegged whiskey on the side.

The particular Saturday night Uncle Jimmy was talking about started out just like all the other Saturday nights had. Daddy had left home that night, promising to be back "in a few minutes." Grandmama and Mama finished cooking Sunday's dinner and went out on the porch while the house cooled. As they sat in the swing relaxing, Mama told Grandmama how dissatisfied she was with Daddy's going out every weekend and leaving her home with two babies. Grandmama had warned her not to crowd Daddy and to give him the opportunity to let off a little steam. Grandmama's words fell on deaf ears. When Daddy wasn't home by midnight, Mama left the house determined to find out exactly what drew him to Ronnie's Café weekend after weekend.

Uncle Jimmy said before Mama married Daddy she had been an exquisite dancer, but when they got married, Daddy asked her to give up dancing. Mama had agreed. Uncle Jimmy suspected that was the reason why Mama was madder than a bat out of hell when she caught Daddy dancing with a lady at Ronnie's Café. Uncle Jimmy said Daddy wasn't actually dancing. He was droping in his knees and grinding his body against the lady's sexual organs. Since Daddy was dancing with his back to the door, he didn't see Mama enter the cafe. Uncle Jimmy said he tried to warn Daddy that Mama was standing right behind him, but Daddy had his eyes closed. He said he even hissed at Daddy, but Daddy was too busy feeling the lady's butt. He was holding a bun in each hand and grinding her rhythmically to the music. Uncle Jimmy couldn't remember what song was playing, but he said Daddy was all into it.

Without saying a word, Mama yanked Daddy off the floor by the back of his collar.

"Oh, L-O-R-D," Daddy screamed as he catapulted through the air and landed face down on the sidewalk.

He had been thrown about ten feet. The impact had knocked the breath out of him. He lay like a rag doll until he became semi-conscious. Then he begged, "Please don't kill me, mister. I didn't know she was married."

The crowd that had been standing frozen in silence went crazy laughing. The laughter seemed to have brought Daddy to full consciousness.

Uncle Jimmy said Mama made a fist and shook it in Daddy's face, threatening to go upside his head with it.

Terrified, Daddy dodged from side to side.

"So this is what you do while I'm stuck home with two babies," Mama roared.

Uncle Jimmy said Daddy started to say something, but before he could say a word Mama said, "Shut up!" She was breathing hard as she struggled to control the sudden urge to kill Daddy.

The crowd formed a circle around Mama and Daddy, hoping to see blood spilled.

"Get up this instant," Mama demanded. "And beat me home."

Without looking up, Daddy obediently went home.

The crowd dispersed, disappointed because they hadn't got to witness Mama spill Daddy's blood. From that night on Daddy stayed home and read the Bible on Saturday nights. It was shortly after that he became a born again Christian. Uncle Jimmy said Daddy had later revealed that he had thought he was going to get killed by the lady's husband or lover. Later, Daddy announced that God had called him to preach the gospel. Uncle Jimmy said there was no room to doubt Daddy's commitment to serving the Lord. Mama had scared the devil out of him!

***

My grandmama was buried today. She had been an inspiring person who spoke softly and displayed her Indian heritage proudly. Her high cheekbones, long silky hair, tall statue, and brilliant mind would have been attributes to flaunt if she had been a worldly person. Unlike others, she was a modest, patient, kind, Christian person who only lived to serve God.

Grandmama always told me she was going to a better home when she left this sinful world, so I know she's happy. I can see her in a special section of Heaven with a big neon sign that flashes "Reserved for Grandmothers Only." In this part of Heaven little elves would be attending to the grandmothers, rushing around frantically, baking moist, fluffy biscuits that melted in their mouths, and cooking chocolate chip cookies and tea cakes.

One elf would be preparing a hot, steamy bath with bubbles floating upward until they kissed the clouds. Another elf would be reading bedtime stories. Beauticians would be on duty to give pedicures, manicures, and hairdos that would boggle the mind! And right in the middle of the pampered ladies would be my grandmama.

***

When I walked into the house today by habit I called out, "Grandmama, I'm home."

I expected her to come down the hall smiling and wiping her hands on her apron as she told me what sweet things we had to eat. She had especially loved to cook desserts. No one could bake like Grandmama. Mama loved her sweet potato pies, but my favorite was her teacakes.

Cake baking time was always a special event that I looked forward to. Grandmama never needed a recipe to cook a cake. She and I would get into the kitchen and mix ingredients. She would tell me how many cups of flour I needed and I would sift them. We didn't have an electric mixer, so we had to beat the batter by hand. She told me to always beat at least three hundred and fifty strokes. Next, I was to test the batter to see how light it was. Then we played it by ear. I would rest, then start anew. We would take turns beating the batter until it was light and airy. Then we would pop the cake into the oven. Our cakes came out perfect every time. Helping to make the cake was only the prelude to the main event—cleaning the bowl! Grandmama and I had an unspoken rule. She never cleaned the bowl. That job was reserved for my brothers and me. Grandmama would leave a little extra batter in the bowl, and we would scrape the bowl clean. My brothers and I took turns cleaning the bowl. If no one was looking, I would scrape the bowl with my fingers, then lick it to be sure I got every drop of batter. It always tasted better that way.

***

Grandmama has been dead for over a month, but I can't get her out of my mind. I think about her day and night. Yesterday in class, I was trying to call Mrs. K. and I yelled out "Grandmama" instead. All the kids gave me a funny look. I apologized to Mrs. K. for calling her the wrong name. That was easier than explaining to the class that I had been sitting there daydreaming about the good times I had shared with my grandmama. There was just no way I could make them understand how much I missed her.

She misses me too. I know she does because she visited me last night. I had gone to bed early because I had a <u>True Romance</u> hidden in the closet. Mama still does not want me to read anything about sex. She says, "Let sleeping dogs lie." According to her, if I read about hugging and kissing, it will make me want to do those things. She said those stories would wake up my hormones. I asked her which ones. She answered, "The wrong ones—the ones that'll make you want babies."

Now if I knew which ones they were, I would destroy them myself. I would never want a baby for myself. You have to change diapers, bathe the babies, listen to a whole lot of crying, and take the little monsters everywhere you go! There's nothing glamorous about that! That's not my plan for living in California. No matter how hard I try, I can't convince Mama to let me read romance stories. She keeps saying, "You'll get into trouble soon enough. Delay unhappiness as long as you can."

I don't want to be sneaky, but she leaves me no choice. All the other girls talk about their boyfriends. All I can talk about is my brothers: "My brothers and I went skating. We went to the movies. We played baseball on the school campus."

Don't get me wrong. I would never tell anyone if I had sex even if I had. Mama always says there are some things you don't tell anyone. I guess sex is one of those things. Besides,

Daddy says having sex outside of marriage is an abomination. He says God will send you straight to hell for that.

Last night I read "Next Door Lover." It was about a teenage girl who called her next door neighbor over every time her mother went somewhere. They had sex on the sofa, floor, her bed, her mother's bed, and even the kitchen table. I decided I had had all I could stand of the story when Jason sprayed whipped cream all over Missy and licked it off. How disgusting!

I turned off the light, closed my eyes, and tried to sleep, but I kept seeing Jason and Missy on the kitchen table. Then I heard someone call me. I sat up. There my grandmother was as plain as day standing at the foot of my bed. She wasn't dressed like an angel. She looked like my grandmother. I was startled, but she must have thought I was scared, because she reached out her hand.

"Don't be frightened," Grandmama said.

I didn't say a word.

"I want you to make me a promise," she continued.

I still didn't say anything.

"Remember to read your Bible daily and be a good girl. Meet me in paradise."

"I—I promise, Grandmama," I said as my thoughts flashed to the story I had been reading. I must have spoken louder than I had intended because Mama yelled, "Go to sleep!"

Then, I heard Mama say, "She's in there talking to Mama."

"Ah," Daddy said. "She's just dreaming."

Before I knew it, the sun was peeping in through half opened blinds.

***

Dear God, please teach me forgiveness. I was wronged today and I responded bitterly. I've grown accustomed to seeing "For Whites Only" signs on public facilities, sitting in the balcony at the movie theater, being served in the kitchen at restaurants, and sitting in the rear on the buses. I'm used to being mistreated by white folks, but how do I deal with discrimination within my own race?

I was proclaimed the best speller in school this year. To get this honor, I sacrificed many hours of recreational time. Whenever I jumped rope or played hopscotch with my playmates, I would mentally spell words to a rhythmic beat. I was obsessed with one idea—bringing the first-place trophy for being the best speller in the district home to my high school.

However, I did not get the opportunity to compete in the district spelling bee today. A new girl named Katie moved to town after I had won the intraschool competition. Her father is a principal and her mother is a teacher. In contrast, my mother substitutes and works in the school lunchroom. My father preaches and works at a local lumberyard.

When I got to school this morning, Mrs. Sutter told me that I would not be the one to represent our school at the district spelling bee. She explained to me that she, along with other teachers, had decided that Katie would have a better chance to win the spelling bee because of her family's academic background. She further explained that I was culturally disadvantaged. I asked her what she meant by this. She said I had not been exposed to many books and had not traveled extensively. I told her I bet I had read more books from the school's library than anyone else in the school. She said that didn't count. The decision had been made.

I tried not to cry, but tears trickled down my face. Lord, I tried not to be disrespectful, but I had studied so hard. When I cried about the months I had wasted studying, Mrs. Sutter just patted me on the back and said, "Now dear, we must not think that way. No learning is ever wasted!"

In my frustration and anger I wanted to slap her, but most of all I wanted Katie to lose the spelling bee. After all, she had not earned the right to compete in the first place. I had! She had stolen my opportunity to be a winner.

Mrs. Sutter allowed me to attend the spelling bee. I sat alone, feeling dejected and thinking about how my mother had sacrificed her money and time to dress me for the occasion. She had made a beautiful skirt and blouse for me at night after cooking and washing dishes all day. I knew my disappointment would break her heart more than it did mine.

I sat anxiously with fingers crossed, praying for Katie to lose. When she misspelled the work "chrysanthemums" during the second round, I cried tears of joy. Sweet vengeance was mine!

Dear God, please help me to understand what happened today. Help me to understand why I feel so rotten. I felt inferior today with my own race. Lord, help me to understand what this incident is trying to teach me. Please help me to become Katie's friend. She didn't have anything to do with what happened today. Give me the strength to keep on pursuing my dreams. Obsess me with fiery passion to succeed. Give me the courage to face life unafraid.

Dear God, bless my Mama too. Help her to forgive my teacher. Mama called her tonight, but Mrs. Sutter didn't apologize. Perhaps she thinks the incident is trivial. Perhaps she doesn't realize that children have feelings too. Perhaps she does not know that culturally disadvantaged people can be heartbroken too. When will she learn?

***

Mrs. Sutter brought me some red and white ribbons today. Mama plaited my hair in three big plaits, a big one in the middle of my head and two in the back. Mrs. Sutter said hair as pretty as mine should have lots of bows on it. She tied bows on each of my plaits. I guess that was her way of trying to make up to me for the way I was treated at the spelling bee. She wasted her money. I don't need presents from her. Besides, I hate wearing ribbons. Mama makes me wear them all the time. I throw the ribbons away and tell Mama I lost them. She gets angry, but she goes to Kress and buys some more. I have a ribbon to match every dress I own! I have enough trouble losing the ribbons Mama buys me. Now I'll have to think of ways to get rid of Mrs. Sutter's. Why doesn't she just say "I'm sorry" and be through with it?

***

If you didn't know any better you would think I've been playing the clarinet all my life. I am now a first chair clarinet player and a soloist oboe player. Can you imagine how good I'll be in a few years?

I'm really good, but sometimes I'm over-confident. Tonight was one of those times. Our school hosted the state drama competition in one-act plays. The band was selected to provide entertainment during intermission. Mr. Miller chose me to play "Humoreske". That's the song I won third place with in state band competition. The entire band was to play the Spanish tune "Ensenada". Previously I had always blown the solo part, but tonight Lester would be playing it. I would be playing the oboe.

Mr. Miller always preached one message as gospel: always count your measures while you are at rest. Whenever we played a new song, I always counted until it was time for me to come back in. After I learned the song, I no longer counted. I relied upon my memory and the melody. It was easy if everyone else came in on time and played his part correctly.

Tonight was a disaster. Lester had never played a solo before. He was nervous, but he didn't tell anyone. Lester and I had a rest at the same time, but he was supposed to start playing a few bars before I did. As usual, I didn't count because I knew when to come in on the melody. Well, to my surprise, when it came time for Lester to come in, he froze. When I looked over at him, he had his mouthpiece in his mouth and the instrument clutched closely to his body. His fingers were moving, but his instrument wasn't making a sound. I knew I was in trouble. Without hearing the melody, I didn't know when to come in. At that time, Mr. Miller did an upbeat with his baton in my direction. I knew that had been the clue for me to begin playing my part, but I had missed it. He gave me one of those "I'll tend to you later" looks.

The trumpets were supposed to come in next, but Gabriel and the others couldn't play because they hadn't been counting either. Like me, they knew when to come in on the melody. They had been counting on me the same way I had been counting on Lester. Nevertheless, Mr. Miller continued to direct "Ensenada". The only sounds heard were the clanging of symbols and an earthy "boomp, boomp" echoing from the bass horn in rhythm with the drums.

The song finally ended and the play competition resumed. I didn't pay any attention as to who was winning the trophies, because I had one thought on my mind—getting out of the band room without Mr. Miller killing me! Everyone else must have had the same thought, because we all scrambled to the band room to put our instruments away. I hadn't wanted to enter the room, but Mr. Miller's rule is that we leave all instruments at school even if a student owns his own instrument. I put up my oboe and had almost made it out the door when I heard an angry voice say, "Get back in here."

I, along with the others, turned around to face what must have been the angriest man alive. I had never seen Mr. Miller lose control before, and we had given him many reasons. Why, he wasn't that upset when during a pre-game show in Jacksonville, Florida, I made our school letter on the home side of the field!

"What do you take me for?" He asked.

No one said a word.

"You made me look like a damn fool!"

Still no one said a word.

For about five minutes he used every curse word he knew while he told us how much we had embarrassed him. When he had satisfied his anger he said, "Get out of here before I lose my religion."

At the sound of those words, we ran for the door. As soon as we were safe on the outside, we giggled. We laughed all the way home and made the symbols, drums, and bass horn sounds.

We stopped laughing before we reached our homes and discussed what had happened. We knew Mr. Miller was wrong for cursing us, but what else could he do? There were too many of us for him to whip, so he gave us a good, old tongue-lashing instead. We agreed that we had heard profanity before, even in our own homes. Besides, we loved Mr. Miller and we had hurt him. It hadn't been done intentionally; nevertheless, we had embarrassed him. There was nothing we could do about what had happened tonight, but we could do better in the future. Before we parted ways, we agreed to never tell our parents about the incident.

We also agreed to live by Mr. Miller's gospel: count, count, count your time while your instrument is at rest!

***

Mama says men are easily fooled. Daddy is no exception. Mama and I went shopping yesterday. We were really just looking around, but I found the neatest pink dress on sale at Mangel's. The sleeves were puffy and had little black bows on each of them. I just had to have it! Mama later fell in love with a Betty Rose suit. The suit had a wrappy tulip jacket, dolman sleeves with adjustable cuffs, and satin lining. Mama said it was a steal at $59.95. She said the suit was looking at her and saying, "Please take me home." She couldn't go home and leave that unhappy suit in the store, so she did what any Christian woman would do. She bought it! Mama and Daddy have an account at the famous store, but she paid cash for it so Daddy wouldn't know she bought it. Mama told me to lock the packages in the trunk. After supper, when Daddy went to lay tile for Mrs. Folsom, Mama and I slipped the packages into the house.

Today started out like any other typical Sunday. Freshly perked coffee perfumed the house. That was our unspoken signal to eat breakfast. Daddy loved to cook breakfast, and Mama appreciated having it cooked for her. But she always worried about Daddy's habit of putting the dishcloth in his back pocket. Mama is afraid that Daddy will mistake it for his handkerchief and blow his nose on it. Whenever possible, I watch Daddy to make sure that never happens.

Breakfast was delicious. Daddy prepared grits, scrambled eggs, and toast. He can't cook biscuits. Mama is the biscuit expert. She can throw some flour, buttermilk, and lard in a bowl, mix the ingredients, knead the dough, and pinch off just enough for a perfect biscuit. It is amazing to me how she can roll the dough around in her left hand, then slap the palm of her right hand in the center and produce perfect biscuits every time.

I admired the biscuits, but I didn't eat any. I don't eat bread. Bread makes you fat, and I don't want to be fat. I did want some coffee, though, but Mama won't let us children drink the stuff. She says coffee will make you black. I've been secretly drinking coffee since I was ten years old, and I haven't seen any change in my complexion.

After breakfast, we hurriedly cleared the table and started getting ready for church. We had to take turns using the bathroom, so I reviewed my Sunday school lesson. I teach a primary class, so I don't have very much to worry about. I just read a card to the children and ask them what they have learned from the lesson. It always makes the parents happy when their little darlings tell them something they've learned—especially the mama's.

Before long it was my turn to use the bathroom and to dress for church. All of us were in different stages of readiness, preparing for the day's services, when I heard Daddy calling us, urging us to hurry because he didn't want to be late. Gabriel, Noah, and Daddy were dressed before Mama and me. As is our custom, they went into the living room to wait for us. It served two purposes. Everyone knew who was ready, and it was a way to hurry up laggers. By coincidence, Mama and I entered the living room at the same time, both wearing our new outfits. I thought Daddy's eyes would pop out of his head!

"Where did you get that new suit?" He asked Mama.

She didn't answer Daddy. Instead, she turned to me and gave me an Academy Award performance.

"What did I tell you, Baby Girl?" She asked in a tone

that suggested I was supposed to know what she was talking about.

I didn't answer, because I didn't know what I was supposed to say.

"I told you your daddy would look at me and think I had on a new suit," she continued. To see the look on her face you would have thought someone had spat in her face.

I nodded, 'Yes." I couldn't tell an outright, blatant lie. I was a Sunday school teacher.

"How long have I had this suit?" She asked me.

"I don't remember," I lied.

"The trouble with you, George, is that you pay no attention to me whatsoever. Why, I could walk out of this house buck naked and you'd never notice!"

Becoming embarrassed, Daddy said, "Candy, settle down. Where's your sense of humor? I was just funning with you. You know I remember that suit. I was just teasing."

After that encounter, Daddy didn't have the nerve to ask about my dress. I guess he was too afraid that it would be an old one that he had forgotten.

As we walked out the door, Mama winked at me and whispered, "It works every time."

I wondered whether Mama had snowed Daddy or whether he was just letting her think she had. Daddy is a special kind of man. He would do anything to make us happy.

CHAPTER 7
NO TRIALS, NO LIFE—1958

I like growing up. Mama gives me more responsibilities. My little brother Matthew will be attending school for the first time this fall. The school system requires that all students be immunized. Today was the day for Matthew to get vaccinated. Mama had to attend to some business for Daddy, so she gave me the responsibility of taking Matthew to the local clinic. Mama didn't want me to go alone because the clinic is across town. Alice's mother said she could go with me. That made me happy, because Alice and I don't get to spend much time together. I'm in the band, chorus, orchestra, teach Sunday school, represent the church on special occasions and still manage to maintain a straight A average in all my classes. Some of the children think Mama and Daddy pressure me to make good grades, but that's not true. Sure they encourage me to always do my best, but I get an unexplainable joy from always having the highest grade in the class. I like being the best. I have never been able to make Alice understand that. She is satisfied making C's, but I can't understand how she can be happy being labeled average. Being average is common. Being average is nothing, but being the best is everything.

That's what Alice and I talked about as we walked Matthew to the clinic. It was so much fun to relive our childhood dreams. Gone are the innocent days when we sat on the ground in my backyard and made dolls from grass stuck in a six ounce Coca-Cola bottle as we dreamed of living in sunny California. There would be no Ku Klux Klan, and the color of our skin wouldn't matter. We would be free! Somehow time has a way of changing things. Now that I'm older, California seems farther away than I ever imagined.

Reliving happy memories made us unaware of how far we had walked. Getting Matthew to the clinic on time was no easy task. Sometimes he ran ahead of us; sometimes he stopped to admire an anthill until we dragged him off. That's the way we completed our trip. After all the pushing and pulling, we finally arrived. Before we entered the building, I straightened his clothes and tried to encourage him. He hated that place, and I knew getting him to take his vaccine would not be easy. He always gave Mama a fit, so I knew what was in store for me. Tears began to roll down Matthew's face as I opened the door to enter the clinic. He pulled back and shouted "No" as loudly as he could.

I jerked his arm a couple of times and said, "Matthew, stop showing out this instant."

The more I jerked him the louder he screamed.

When I saw I wasn't going to get anywhere that way, I leaned down and said, "Matthew you're getting ready to start school. That means you're a big boy. Big boys don't cry. Have you ever seen Daddy, Noah, or Gabriel cry?"

He shook his head to indicate "no".

"That's right," I continued. "And you will never see them cry. They're big boys and big boys don't let anyone see them cry, especially girls."

As young as he is that message seemed to get through to him. Yes, Matthew would grow up to be the typical male. Convinced that I had it made, I opened the door, went to the sign-in desk, and took a number. It seemed that everyone had waited until the last minute to get their children immunized. The colored people's side is dingy-looking and decorated with straight chairs. A few broken and dirty toys are strewn around for the children to play with. Our side is separated from the white folks which, in contrast, has comfortable chairs, freshly painted walls, and an abundance of magazines and toys.

I didn't want Matthew to play with the toys, but I was willing to do anything to keep him occupied. He played until he got tired. I sat him on my lap to comfort him. Actually, I needed comforting more than he did. I wondered why Mama brought Matthew to that clinic. Those people are so different from us. Most of them don't even speak standard English. Mama always made us use it. Why didn't they? A lady struck up a conversation with me. I answered her back, but I did not say another word to her. To be certain she did not bother me again, I pretended to doze off. Sitting so long with my eyes closed, I actually did take a nap. Matthew's laughter woke me up.

"Look, Sister," he said, pointing to a crying boy who had just left the nurse. "He's crying. He's not a big boy."

"No, he's not," I agreed, thankful that Matthew was going to march into the room and take his shot like a little man.

Matthew continued to sit on my lap and laugh at everyone who came back to the waiting room crying. Finally, our number was called. Matthew jumped off my lap and headed toward the room. This is going to be a piece of cake, I told myself. The nurse told me to take a seat in a chair near her desk. She asked me a few questions about Matthew. Then she filled out his immunization chart. I noticed that Matthew had begun to squirm a little, but I had no idea what was about to happen. The nurse turned her back to us as she filled the needle. When she turned around, the needle was right in front of Matthew's eyes. I thought they would pop out of his head! He jumped from my lap, knocking over trays and other supplies as he ran from the room. He ran down the hall, and we ran after him. We finally cornered him in a supply room and dragged him back kicking and screaming.

He got his shot, and I got a lecture. The nurse told me to tell Mama to bring him herself the next time he needed a booster. She said she was too busy to chase down kids to give them something they needed. She even added that Mama might want to take him to our private physician. That way he wouldn't have to wait so long and get nervous. No matter what she said, she made it clear that she never wanted to see us again!

Chasing Matthew had been embarrassing, but it had also been fun. He was not a big boy and had showed me that it was all right to be "five going on six." That's the way he always answers anyone who asks him his age. In a way he had been a big boy. He had not wanted to be vaccinated and had let everyone know it. I wonder whether I'll have the courage to be as brave about other matters in my life as Matthew was about his shot. It's something to think about.

***

My brother Noah got an awful whipping tonight. He and his friend Turnip Head stole a car. Actually, they just borrowed it for a few hours. The owner had left the car at the high school to be repaired by the auto mechanics class.

Noah and Turnip Head went joy riding. They returned the car, but Lester told on them. Lester was with them when they found the keys in the car, but he wouldn't ride with them. Noah called Lester "chicken." That made Lester mad, so he went home and told his mama. Lester's mama called my mama.

When Noah got home, Daddy had a big switch waiting for him. It was really several small switches plaited together. Mama had told Daddy to whip Noah. Following Mama's orders, Daddy marched him into the back bedroom and told him to undress. Daddy placed a ladder back chair in the center of the room and told Noah to lie face down across the chair with his behind in the air. Sounds of switches beating against bare flesh could be heard along with Daddy shouting his sacrifices.

"I work hard for you. I do without so you can have things I never had. Do you care? No!" Daddy answered himself.

"Do you show any appreciation? No! What do you do? You go out and steal a car. This is the thanks I get!"

"Please don't hit me again," Noah begged. "I won't do it no more."

"I know you won't," Daddy said. "When I get through with you," as the switch struck him again and again.

I cried for Noah. His pleading cries were worse than receiving the licks myself.

Daddy yelled at Noah, "Shut up. I'm not hurting you."

For the life of me, I couldn't understand how he could expect Noah not to cry when he was beating the hell out of him.

On command the screams changed to whimpers and loud grunts. The beating was over.

"Now put on some clothes," Daddy admonished, "and don't ever let me hear tell of you doing something like that again, or I'll give you something worse than what you just got."

Daddy left the room.

I peeped thought the keyhole. Noah was still draped limply over the chair sobbing. He slid his right hand across his nose, wiping it with one swift movement. He rose from the chair and dressed hurriedly. He stood still a few minutes and looked around the room. He gave his pant buckle a hunch, lifted his head, and walked out of the room as though nothing had happened.

I will never steal a car. I could never take a whipping like Noah did. I'd rather die. Daddy explained to Noah that he had whipped him because he loved him. After their talk, Noah and Daddy seemed to have established an unexplainable bond.

***

Mama took us to the Dosta Theater today to see "Teacher's Pet." Usually she stays at home, but she wanted to see her idol, Clark Gable. Although he is fifty-seven, Mama still finds him handsome and irresistible. She said he still has charm and sex appeal. He just looks like an old white man to me! Mama especially likes Clark Gable because she met Daddy at one of his movies. How she loves to tell the story of their first meeting. He had walked her home that night and told her how he had seen her in his dreams as his wife. She said she laughed in his face and called him silly, but they were married by the justice of the peace a year later.

The night she met Daddy, she had gone to the refreshment stand to buy popcorn during intermission. As she approached the counter, she saw the most handsome man standing before her. He had sideburns and a neatly trimmed mustache. She had found her bronze Clark Gable.

***

I find the news both depressing and unbelievable. Martin Luther King was stabbed. When I first heard the news, I was certain he had been stabbed by a white person. But, to my surprise, the stabber was a colored woman. The news reporter described her as being deranged. That's the only thing that can describe the situation. How can someone try to murder a man who is willing to sacrifice his life for others? I truly love and admire Martin Luther King. He tries to fulfill one of God's greatest commandments: "Love your neighbor as I have loved you." He loves all people regardless of race, color, or creed. I pray that he doesn't die. There's so much he can do for mankind.

***

There's magic in the air, and thanks to my little brother Matthew, I get to be a part of the fantasy. He's almost six years old now, and he understands that Santa Claus brings presents to all good boys and girls. Matthew had me write a letter to Santa, telling him how good he had been all year. Then he had me make a list of all the toys he wanted: a train, cowboy suit, gun and holster, football, basketball, and a pair of skates. Being born after Daddy had reached middle life made Matthew the apple of his eye. There was no way on earth that Matthew would not receive everything he asked for. But to Mama and Daddy's amazement, Matthew's list didn't end with his wishes. He asked me to write down what I wanted Santa Claus to bring me. My list was even longer than his. I wrote down everything I could imagine: stockings, pocketbooks, shoes, dresses, books, a coat with an unattached hood, dolls, and an umbrella. My list went on and on. I was only playing make-believe with Matthew because I knew I was too old to believe in Santa.

When we finished the letter, Matthew took it to Mama to mail to Santa. He wanted to be sure the letter had enough time to get to the North Pole. Mama read the letter aloud. She was amused until she came to my wish list.

She looked at my little brother and said, "Santa is going to do everything in his power to get you everything on the list, but he'll have to pass your sister by."

Tears welled up in Matthew's eyes. "Why can't Santa bring Sister some toys too?"

"She's too old for Santa," Mama replied.

Matthew fell out on the floor crying. "If she can't have nothing, then I don't want nothing."

He refused to eat dinner and cried until Mama assured him I would receive presents from Santa just like he would.

"Can she leave him a piece of cake too?" Matthew asked.

"Why not?" Mama said to reassure him.

After Mama had tucked Matthew into bed, she called me aside to talk with me. She explained that she was going along with playing Santa with me because she did not want to disappoint Matthew. She told me to find an excuse for not sending Santa a list next Christmas. Besides, my wish list had been too long. I explained that I had not expected to receive everything I had written on the list. I had been fantasizing about all the things I would buy if I had the money. Mama said no harm had been done and closed the matter.

I wish I had called her back into the room to let her know that I was really looking forward to Christmas this year. Last year's celebration had been boring. Mama and Daddy had given each of us older children the same amount of money to shop with. We chose our own gifts, but something was missing. I like not knowing what I'm going to receive. Even if I've asked for a special gift, I want to be surprised by the color or any unexpected item. It can be something as small as a stuffed stocking. I like to be surprised, and Christmas is the best time of the year for welcomed surprises.

***

There is something mystical about the Christmas holidays. At any other time, Noah would have pouted longer about not receiving as many pairs of socks as Gabriel did, but this time was different. On Christmas morning, Noah acted as if nothing had happened; instead, he seemed more cheerful than ever. The days immediately following Christmas Noah visited classmates who had gone on to other colleges and universities only to be disappointed. They often found themselves trapped in the "my school is better than yours" debate. On the other hand, when he visited his classmates who had decided against furthering their education, he often found himself the target of ridicule. Noah had always used correct grammar (our parents would accept nothing less), yet because he was attending college, he was accused of showing off his knowledge and acting white.

Gabriel said after the experiences he had during Christmas break he could now put some of Daddy's religious teaching in perspective. I asked him what he meant by that.

"Do you remember Matthew 7:6?" Noah asked.

I shook my head to indicate that I didn't.

He went to the bookshelf and brought back the family Bible. He found the passage quickly and read aloud, "Give not that which is holy unto the dogs, neither cast ye your pearls before swine, lest they trample them under their feet, and turn again and rend you."

He slammed the Bible shut.

"I've been talking to a bunch of idiots," he said. He disagreed aloud with himself, giving me no chance to express my opinion. He continued, "No, I think they know better, but it's easier to make fun of me than to try to better themselves. Well, I'm not throwing any more pearls after swine. If they're contented with nothing, so be it. Now you, little sister, are another story."

He gave me one of those hugs that shouted, "I love you!"

After that conversation, we spent the rest of his vacation talking about Tuskegee. It was like another world to him, and he had found his place. His head was bursting with knowledge and new ideas that he was dying to share, and I became his audience. He introduced me to a new way of thinking. According to his professors, there was so much wrong with the way we were being taught in school.

For example, Noah said our teachers should not have had us singing "Dixie" in school. When I told him I liked the words to the song, he became angry with me and accused me of being brainwashed. He asked me to explain why I would "live and die in Dixie."

I thought about his question for a while, but I could not think of anything that I thought he wanted to hear. After a period of silence, Noah asked, "Now do you see what I'm talking about?" He added, "It's all the white man's lie. He wants to delude you into thinking that you have a wonderful life in the South when you are actually just accepting his leftovers like a dog taking scraps from a table."

"It's not as bad as you make it sound, Noah."

"It's not?" He gave me one of those knowing looks that said, "I've got you now!" "Why do you have to sit in the balcony at the movies?"

I made no attempt to answer.

"Why do we have to ride in the rear of the bus?"

No answer.

"Why is it that you can't go into a restaurant, sit down, order a meal, and enjoy your dinner like any other human being?"

By now I knew he didn't expect me to answer. He was just giving me something to think about. I remembered that Mrs.

Sutter had called them rhetorical questions. He was teasing my brain, but I knew Noah had never been more serious in his life.

"Do you still want to live and die in Dixie?"

"No," I said, somewhat ashamed.

Perhaps that had been the perfect time to tell him about my dream of going to California. I respected Noah, and if he had told me that wasn't the thing to do, I would have abandoned the whole idea and I wasn't ready to do that.

"While we're changing the world, tell me what else you don't like," I said.

His face lit up again as he shared his ideas with me.

"I know you're still a child," he began, but he corrected himself when he saw the resentment on my face.

"Let me start over," he said. "I know this is all new to you, so I'm just going to give you a few more things to think about. When you've accepted my ideas totally, I want you to share them with your friends." Teasing me, he asked, "You do have some intelligent friends?"

I gave him a playful punch in the stomach.

"Think about the name of our race. I remember being called colored. What does colored mean? Red, blue, green, purple, brown, black, orange—all these are colors. Have you ever seen a purple person? No, and you never will. Next we were called Negroes. Many whites like that name because they can easily confuse the pronunciation with nigger. Do you know what we should be called?"

He didn't wait for me to answer.

"Afro-American," he said proudly.

I thought I knew a little history and tried to impress Noah.

"All Negroes didn't come from Africa," I told him.

"We'll discuss that later," Noah said. "We have a proud heritage. We are descended from kings and queens. That's what the white man doesn't want you to know. He doesn't want you to know that royal blood flows through your veins. You see, if you know who you are and love who you are it will be harder to 'keep you in your place'."

Noah and I talked until it was time for bed. I was able to grasp some of the things he told me, because I had been unhappy about so many incidents that had happened in my life. I understood the racial prejudice, but I didn't understand the cruelty I had received from some of my classmates and teachers because I was dark-skinned. After our conversation I felt a little better about myself. It was alright to be dark. I was of African descent. I might even be of royal descent. There was no doubt—I was!

That night before I went to bed, I thanked God for Noah's taking the time to share what he was learning in college. I thanked Mama and Daddy for being unselfish and sending him to college. I thanked his teachers for having the foresight to get a job at a school where they could voice their opinions without fear of being fired. Before I closed my eyes, I swore I would never sing ""Dixie" again, and I would identify my race as Afro-American. After all, doesn't the Bible say, "As a man thinketh in his heart, so is he?"

CHAPTER 8
TROUBLED TIME—1959

School was dismissed early today. Girls were screaming and fainting everywhere. Our classmate Alicia committed suicide yesterday, but most of us didn't know until we arrived at school this morning. The boys choked back tears. Alicia had been so pretty. She had peachy skin dotted with freckles. She looked like the white ladies did in the magazines, but there was one exception—she was a little chubby. She didn't have a Lana Turner shape. Maybe that was why Lawrence didn't want to marry her.

We were all surprised to hear that Alicia had killed herself because of Lawrence, especially me. I though she was going to marry my cousin Mark. He worshipped the ground she walked on. He couldn't talk without saying her name. I have never seen anyone so crazy about a person in my life. I thought they were sexually active, but Mark said she wouldn't let him touch her. He told me they had French kissed a few times, but she wouldn't let him go any further. When I asked him how to French kiss, he told me that you suck each other's tongue as far down your throat as you can without gagging. The idea sounded repulsive to me, but I decided it must be something you're supposed to do when you're in love.

Mark said Alicia was the kind of girl a man should respect. He didn't want to pressure her into doing anything she didn't want to do because he wanted to marry her. He was so glad he had Alicia. He loved her with all his heart. Now she's dead. Her mother found her body hanging from a beam in a bedroom. "Come to me" was playing in the background.

When I came home from school, I found my records scattered over my bed. Mama had been looking for the record. Alicia had thrown a rope over the beam, stood on a chest of drawers, and jumped off. A letter on the dresser explained why she had killed herself. She was pregnant. She had told Lawrence, but he had insisted that the baby wasn't his. Having a baby out of wedlock was a no-no. She didn't want to disgrace her family, so she did the honorable thing—killed herself.

Shirlie, Alice, and I discussed suicide. We all agreed we would have done the same thing. Mama always said if I swallowed a pumpkin seed I would have to quit school and get a job. Ugh! The thought of a job is enough, but how would I be able to afford my trip to California? Besides, I don't want a baby. I don't know anyone who does except maybe Aunt Judy! Her baby died while she was giving birth. It happened years ago, but she still talks about it. She says she has always wanted children, but who knows? Grownups say one thing and end up doing something else.

There's so much I do not know or understand. Does an unborn baby go to hell when the mother commits suicide? I'll pray for the baby's soul.

***

Gnats and mosquitoes have infested our lives and so has adversity. Mama said it was bound to happen. She wished she had listened to her own mind and not let Gabriel play in a band. At first everything was fine. Daddy picked up Gabriel like clockwork after each gig. We all sat up until he came home. The managers would let him bring leftovers home. We never knew what we would get. That's how I developed my passion for caviar.

Gabriel said all rich people eat it whether they like it or not. If you wanted to be sophisticated you couldn't let anyone know you didn't like caviar. It was a delicacy. No matter how long I stared at it, caviar still looked like fish eggs to me. Nevertheless, I concluded that Gabriel must have known what he was talking about, so I acquired a taste for it.

After a while, Daddy got tired of driving Gabriel's band home. Mama said Gabriel should get out of the band if he wasn't going to have adult supervision. Daddy told Mama that she had to trust Gabriel. Gabriel said he was no longer a child and could provide his own transportation home. At first he came home at the usual time. Then he got later and later. Mama told Daddy to check on Gabriel, but Daddy said Mama didn't have enough to worry about, so she was creating her own problems.

I didn't know what was going on, but I knew something was wrong. Gabriel stopped bringing home hors'derves, and I was left with an insatiable craving for caviar. He no longer told us disgraceful stories about prominent citizens. I was surprised to learn that Lawyer Binion was openly having an affair. Gabriel said he also was an alcoholic. One night he came in with a prostitute. Well, Gabriel said that's what she *looked* like. She got so drunk until she threw up all over the floor. Lawyer Binion tried to help her out of the restaurant without everyone knowing what was going on, but he had trouble staggering to the car himself.

No, Gabriel didn't tell stories like that anymore. In fact, he became distant and secretive. We were wondering what was wrong with him. We didn't have to wonder long because at two a.m. on a Sunday morning Detective Houser knocked on our door. He wanted to search the house. He accused Mama and Daddy of hiding stolen goods. They tried to tell him they didn't know what he was talking about, but he insisted they did. Between his calling us niggers, spades, coons, and jungle bunnies, we learned that Gabriel had been arrested for attempted burglary. The information we got was that he, Red, and Daniel were in an alley behind a store when the police came around to check the buildings. They tried to run, but they got caught. Gabriel had a crowbar in his possession and no plausible reason for having it.

Mama and Daddy went to the jail the next morning to bail Gabriel out. The desk sergeant told them he had been denied bail. That made Mama and Daddy furious. You would think Gabriel had murdered someone! They turned to Lawyer Binion for help. He may be a lover of loose women, but he's a damn good lawyer. He's known for defending colored people. It's rumored around town that he has a colored mistress. The word is her house is full of antiques, and she eats out of fine china, not just on Sundays but everyday of the week. If anyone would help Gabriel, we were sure Lawyer Binion would.

The next morning they were in his office as soon as it opened for business. Mama and Daddy told him what had happened. He remembered Gabriel and admired his playing.

Agreeing to represent Gabriel, he said, "That boy plays a mean horn, and I want to hear him play it again."

We came home confident that Gabriel would be home before noon. Noon came and went. We ate lunch without Gabriel. Time passed slowly. Finally, it was time to eat dinner. We ate dinner without Gabriel. Daddy tried to be optimistic as he prayed, but we knew he was just trying to be brave for our sake. We knew he had cause to worry. We knew a colored man's life didn't mean anything to a white man. I had seen a policeman kill a colored man in cold blood. It had happened when I was only six years old, but the memory was as vivid as if it had happened yesterday.

We lived next to Mr. Henry Buckle's store. There was a bench outside where colored men sat around and talked. On the day of the murder, an old man dressed in overalls was lying on the bench. The policeman went over to the bench and shook him. I don't remember what they said, but I remember the policeman told the old man to run. At first the old man refused. Then the policeman shouted, "I said run, nigger!" The old man obeyed. Shots rang out. The old man's lifeless body fell to the ground. The next day I heard Mama and Daddy say an article in the newspaper stated he had been killed resisting arrest. That was the end of that.

Now, as I think back on the incident, I see someone shouting in slow motion in an inhuman voice. I recognized the policeman, older and stouter, but it was the same man who came to search our house—Detective Houser. The man was a cold-blooded killer.

We tried to keep life as close to normal as humanly possible. We passed the hours staring at the television screen. I won't say we saw anything specifically because I couldn't keep my mind off Gabriel. The only thing I remember about "Wagon Train" was the Ward Bond shouting, "Wagons, ho!" Gabriel's safety occupied my thoughts and prayers. I knew that he could be killed at any minute, and no one would give a damn. It wasn't right. It wasn't fair!

Around midnight, Mama told us to go to bed. Her usual instructions are to go to bed and go to sleep, but she knew that would be asking for the impossible. However, I must have dozed off because I remember being awakened by the telephone's ringing. I, along with Mama, Daddy, and Noah got out of bed. Mama answered the telephone. It was Detective Houser! He told her he would let Gabriel out of jail if she would come to the station and have sex with him and his friends. Mama told him that Gabriel would just have to rot in jail. Mama had called Detective Houser's bluff. The next day he turned Gabriel loose. There was no trial—nothing!

Life had been restored to its simpler state. Gabriel no longer plays in the jazz band, and I don't eat caviar anymore.

***

Summers in South Georgia can be pretty boring if you don't amuse yourself. I've tried very hard to keep busy. I've read lots of poetry and even tried to write some. Somehow my poems never match the emotion of Shelley, Keats, or Byron. I've fallen in love with Shakespeare. My how he can write! I enjoyed reading "Anthony and Cleopatra" and "Othello", but his sonnets eighteen and twenty-nine captured my spirit and soul. I have never heard anyone express the power of love the way he does. Is it possible that I will find someone who will love me spiritually?

Mama says life is not like what I read in books and see in movies. I don't want reality. I want romance. I want to be able to write a love poem from my experiences like Emily Barret Browning. It can happen. I know it can if I believe hard enough. What's wrong with dreaming?

I've also been reading factual materials. I've almost completed our set of The Book of Knowledge. There are so many questions I want to answer. Why is the sky blue? Who created God? If Adam and Eve were the first two people on earth, where did their children's husbands and wives come from? What makes the seasons change? How do the birds know when to migrate south? Like the wonders of nature, human beings baffle me.

I have been having sleepless nights because Ralph, Charles, and Leon did something stupid. They must not have had enough to keep them busy because the radio announcer stated that they robbed a service station on Highway 41. They were caught a few hours later. The next day the same announcer said Charles was dead. He allegedly hanged himself in jail. We all doubted that, but we had no proof and no one really investigated the incident. I guess they had worn everybody out. They have been in some kind of trouble since elementary school. They were devilish, but they never hurt anyone.

Charles' death really disturbed me, because we have gone to the same church as long as I can remember. We were in the same Sunday school class, studied the same Bible, and sang in the choir. I knew it was wrong to go out and take something that didn't belong to you. Why didn't Charles? Daddy said that incident just proved that you can lead a horse to water, but you can't make him drink. He said it all boils down to what a person's thirsty for. This summer I was thirsty for knowledge, but Charles, Ralph, and Leon had been thirsty for excitement. They got more than they bargained for. Ralph and Leon will be sent away, and Charles will be buried. Charles' death will be hard to overcome because I'll see his mother and sister every Sunday at church. I'm really worried about how to act and what to say. Should I even say anything at all? What words are there to solder (my new vocabulary word) a broken heart? It's not like he died in an accident or from a long illness. I pray that the right words will come to me at the proper time.

CHAPTER 9
MY TURN—1960

I can't believe it! I'm finally a senior. I will soon be able to shake the dust of this antiquated town from my shoes and travel to unknown places. Why am I so disappointed? For some reason I expected life to be different, but everything is the same. I'm around the same people. I know what they're going to talk about, and they know what I'm going to talk about. I know more interesting things to talk about, but if I talk about a topic that my classmates know little or nothing about, they laugh at me and accuse me of making things up. I'm an avid reader; they're not, not even my best friends Shirlie and Alice. So I'm stuck listening to the same conversations. A favorite topic is how much everyone is going to miss this town and everyone here. There must be something wrong with me because I don't anticipate missing anyone. Why should I? They never made me a part of their groups anyway. I was always the bookworm that they came to when they wanted help with their schoolwork. Never once did they invite me to a birthday party! When I told them about it, they said I would have been invited, but they didn't think my parents would let me attend. I couldn't harbor any ill feelings because there was some truth in their reasoning. Nevertheless, they should have invited me and given me the opportunity to tell them I couldn't come. Besides, you can never guess what grownups are going to do

There is one part of high school I will miss—the band.

I love marching and playing music, especially at concerts. No matter where I live, music will always be a special part of my life. Being in the chorus is fun too. It would be more fun if I could sing. I don't have a beautiful voice, but I can harmonize. I guess you can say I'm one of those people who make the chorus look big. Everything has a purpose and a value. I learned why I joined the chorus. A gorgeous, I mean drop dead gorgeous, boy joined the chorus today. All the girls kept sniggling and whispering about him. He transferred from a school in Mississippi. His voice is so silky. I could listen to him sing twenty-four hours a day. My favorite gospel group is the Harmonizing Four. For his audition, the new boy sang "Motherless Child" and "Go Down Moses". He sounded just like Jimmy Jones, the bass singer who made those tunes classics. All the girls were spellbound. The boys tried to act indifferent, but it was easy to tell that they were more than a little concerned about the newcomer who was getting all the attention that had been usually reserved for them. The handwriting was on the wall. They would have to clean up their acts. We had someone else to give our attentions to.

Actually, I never paid them too much attention anyway, but I intend to get to know this new fellow. I like him. I think he is interested in me because he smiled at me as we were leaving class. It was one of those smiles that say "Hey, I'd like to get to know you better." I wonder if he likes to read. Until I find out more about him, I'll listen to the Harmonizing Four and dream about him.

"Sometimes I feel like a motherless child, a long way from home."

***

My fantasy lover's name is David, the most beautiful name

in the whole wide world! I've whispered it, shouted it, and even prayed it. No matter how I've said it, it is music to my ears. He asked for my telephone number. Shirlie told me not to get my hopes up. She said he's probably heard that I've never had a boyfriend, so he's looking for fresh meat. I told Shirlie that she was just jealous because he didn't ask for her number. She's used to having all the boys flirt with her. She's bright but not that pretty. I must admit she does have something on me; she has to wear a bra. I don't because I'm flat-chested. Mama buys me falsies. You know the little contoured rubber pads that you stuff into the bra itself. I don't enjoy wearing them, but Mama said they make my clothes fit better. No one will ever know unless I get married, and that's a long ways off. What does Shirlie know anyway? She's not a love expert. Besides, she can't even pass chemistry. If she hurts my feelings again, I'm not going to help her with her homework.

I'm so anxious for David to call me. I did something stupid today. I called him. I didn't actually call him because I didn't talk to him. When I rang his number, he answered the telephone. He said hello several times. I stood silent on the other end. I wanted to talk to him, but Mama says no decent, self-respecting girl calls a man first. You always act disinterested, like they're persuading you to do something you really don't want to do, but at the same time, you're leading them to slaughter. I'm not sure I agree with this strategy. I think if two people care about each other, they should be honest and up front with each other. Why waste time playing games?

I guess Mama knows what she's talking about, because Daddy is truly devoted to her. In fact, Daddy says she is the only woman he has ever loved. It must be nice having no competition. I don't expect my life to be like that. I'm built like Olive Oyl and the most exciting thing I do is read.

I wonder if Shirlie is right.

***

David did call, again and again. He finally got up enough nerve to walk me home. Mama was in the kitchen mopping the floor. David took the mop from her hand and insisted she let him finish the job. He won her trust with that single act of chivalry. Now he courts the whole family. Every family activity is planned with him in mind. I don't even have to be home for him to come over and stay for hours. He is comfortable with all members of the family, including Daddy. They both like to sing, so it is not surprising for David to stay late and sing with Daddy for hours. Everyone takes if for granted that we will marry one day. I don't want to rush into anything because I've never dated before, and I'm not sure how you're supposed to feel when you're in love.

David asked me if I felt anything when we kissed. I told the truth and admitted that I get a tingling feeling all over my body when we kissed. He said that's my nature telling me that I want to have sex with him. He makes me so angry when he talks nasty. He says there is nothing nasty about sex between two people who love each other. At those times I remind him that sex is reserved for married people. He says he knows that, but he gets physically ill, even down to having pain in his groin area. I shut my emotions down and send him home. He knows I want to leave this town and try to find a better life for myself. He wants me to stay here and have a baby. I don't think so.

David and I have an on-again off-again romance. I liked it before it got complicated. The truth of the matter is we spend too much time together. I never have any time for myself. He is here all the time. I don't understand how his mother lets him stay away from home so much. When I do ask him to go home, he tells me that he did not come to see me. He came over to help my daddy or mama do this or that. I don't like having him around so much because he acts as if he owns me. He gets angry if I talk to other boys at school. They were my friends before I met him, and I don't understand why I should give up their friendships. He goes to church with us on Sunday, and he's no different there. He's beginning to get on my nerves.

Tonight I betrayed my parent's trust. They left David and me at home alone while they went to the hospital to see Mrs. Blue, a member of the senior choir. We were in my room putting a puzzle together, so Mama just stuck her head in the door and told us they were going to the hospital and would be back shortly. Daddy reminded David to take care of me.

Matthew came running and shouting, "Can I go? I want to go too."

"All right, "Mama said. "You can come along."

That left David and me alone. I knew the fun was over for the evening. He was going to talk about his favorite subject— sex. Before they had even gotten the car out of the driveway he was reaching for me. I pushed the puzzle at him, sending pieces everywhere.

"Look what you've done," he said.

I reminded him that all I wanted to do was finish the puzzle.

"All right," he said. "If you don't want to kiss me I'll just have to find someone who does."

"I never said I didn't want to kiss you, but you try to go too far."

He clasped his hands behind his back and asked, "Will you kiss me now? I'm helpless. Just an itsy bitsy kiss?"

"Just a little one," I agreed as I moved closer to him.

At first he brushed his lips lightly against mine. It felt so right. Then he slowly parted my lips with his tongue, thrusting it down my throat, then out again. I was beginning to feel that tingling again as he squeezed my breast. I realized he was doing it again—ruining a perfect evening by being selfish. I began to struggle with him as he begged me to take off my panties. The more he begged the harder I struggled. Being more powerful than me, he managed to throw me on the bed and lay on top of me.

"I won't hurt you," he promised, rubbing his fully clothed body against mine.

I just lay there like a log waiting for him to finish whatever he had started. His breathing became louder as he continued to rub his body against mine. Soon heavy breathing was replaced with loud grunts as I felt his body shake above me. Then all was quiet. He gave me a long, painful squeeze as he simultaneously kissed me on the nose.

"I love you," he said as he hopped from the bed and busied himself by picking up the puzzle pieces.

We didn't talk anymore that night. There was nothing else to say. We had crossed the line of innocence into the territory of experience. It would just be a matter of time before we gave in to all our desires and curiosity.

***

Autumn is my favorite time of year. Trees full of orange and brown leaves, sprinkled with green reminders decorate the streets. The weather is cool enough to be comfortable without air conditioning, but still warm enough to enjoy a walk into town.

Mama and I took one of our customary walks. Mama

did most of the talking. I wanted to tell her about David, but I didn't want to disappoint her. He is the first boy she has ever welcomed into her home and treated the same way she treats her own sons. Any bad news would hurt her, therefore, I kept my shame to myself while she shared past experiences with me. I discovered Mama had a sense of humor and deep convictions.

The first story Mama told me was about Daddy. She lives to talk about Daddy. She has always told me that a person talks about what is in his heart and mind. As much as she talks about Daddy, I can tell he has the most special place in her heart.

"Did I ever tell you about the day your Daddy bought his navy blue pinstripe suit?"

"I was with him when he bought it," I replied.

"No, you were not. Mr. Leland gave you children money to go to the ice cream parlor."

"That's right," I said, remembering the chocolate ice cream I had bought.

She continued, "Your daddy looked at every suit in the store before he finally settled on the navy blue pin striped suit. Mr. Leland didn't have his size, so he offered your daddy a discount on any other suit in the store, but your daddy only wanted the navy blue pinstriped suit. Mr. Leland finally gave in and said," Alright, George, if that's the suit you want, you shall have it." He took your daddy to a dressing room where they stayed for quite some time.

Mama said Daddy emerged later wearing a suit that was three sizes too large for him. He was holding up the pants to keep from walking on the hem. Mr. Leland led Daddy to a mirror. When Daddy got almost in front of it, she said Mr. Leland grabbed the coat in the back.

"See how it fits you," he told Daddy.

From the front view the fit looked perfect. Daddy was pleased.

"Let me see how it fits in the back," he said.

While Daddy was turning his back toward the mirror and looking over his shoulder, Mr. Leland grabbed the coat in the front, giving the back a perfect fit.

Mama said she laughed so hard until pain pierced her side. Of course, Daddy bought the suit and Mama later had it altered. Just recalling the incident brought tears to her eyes. She explained, "It's one of those incidents where you have to be there to really appreciate the story."

We walked alone in silence. I had read in <u>The Book of Knowledge</u> that an individual's mind is never vacant. We think about something all the time. I wondered what Mama was thinking about. I was thinking about David. Do I continue to see him or do I walk away? He had violated me, not physically, but mentally and spiritually. He wanted me to give him what I was not ready to give any man, yet he had found a cheap way of satisfying his desires. Was I still a virgin? I wondered.

Mama broke the silence. "Did I tell you about the time your daddy was silly enough to keep some moonshine for a lady?"

Before I could answer she launched into another story. Mama said Miss Lottie lived next door. She was old, and she used her age as an advantage. She called Daddy her son and always told him how dependent she was on him. She had Daddy believing she would die if he didn't cut wood for her, run her errands, and so on. Mama said she was setting him up for the big kill.

Mama said one night while she was taking a bath, someone knocked on the door. Later when she asked Daddy who had been at the door, he told her it had been Miss Lottie. She had wanted him to keep a package for her. Mama said she didn't ask Daddy what the package was. Days later she noticed Daddy acting strangely. She also noticed him darting in and out of a room that was only used for storage. On one of his visits to the room, Mama followed him and discovered him sipping from a gallon of moonshine.

Mama said she was livid and told Daddy to make Miss Lottie keep her own liquor. She reminded Daddy that if the moonshine was found in the house he would be sent to jail, not Miss Lottie. Daddy assured Mama that no one would ever suspect an elderly deaconess who punctuated every sentence with "Praise be the Lord." Well, Mama said two days later the sheriff raided Miss Lottie's house. They didn't find anything because the moonshine was at their house. Mama said if the sheriff had come to their house, he would have arrested Daddy on sight. Daddy was shaking and perspiring. When the sheriff left Miss Lottie's house, Mama said Daddy went over to her house and told her to come get her moonshine or he would pour it out.

I laughed at the comical picture Mama had painted of Daddy. I also laughed at Miss Lottie because Mama said Daddy had poured water into the moonshine to replace what he had drunk. Anyway, Daddy learned a valuable lesson and so did Mama. She said if anyone ever asks Daddy to keep moonshine again, she will pour it out herself and face the consequences.

Somehow our conversation shifted from Daddy to one of our neighbors. I could tell that Mama was seeing me as a more mature person because she talked about love and betrayal—things she never mentioned before. Our neighbors had had an awful fight. Mr. Lee's girlfriend's mother died, and he went to the funeral and sat with the family. Mr. Lee's daughter also attended the funeral. She had heard rumors that he would be there, and to her dismay, he marched in with his girlfriend's arm wrapped around his.

His daughter went home immediately after the funeral and told her mother. Her mother burst into tears, but she didn't say anything. We all knew she was afraid of her husband because he beat her the same way he beat his children. Unlike her mother, the daughter jumped into action. She made trip after trip outside, throwing her father's clothes in the trash pile shouting, "I'm tired of him treating my Mama this way! I'm tired of it!"

Luckily, her father was at his girlfriend's house consoling her and did not know what his daughter was doing. Her older brother happened to come home before their father and returned their father's belongings to their proper places in the bedroom. Mama said if she had been his wife, she would have thrown him and his things out.

I learned so much about Mama today. Even though she always appears to be in control, she understands hurt and disappointment. It is reassuring to know that Mama has feelings too; she just keeps them locked deep inside. The talks we share make me love Mama more and more.

***

Mama and Daddy had a terrible fight last night. I was thankful that Cousin Ruth was visiting us. After dinner Daddy sent me to the store to get a pack of cigarettes. Like the man in the commercial, he'd walk a mile for a Camel. As usual, Mama and Cousin Ruth were hustling about the kitchen preparing today's meal: turnip greens, baked hen, corn bread dressing, and chocolate cake. The enticing aroma permeated the house, whetting our appetites. The meal had to be prepared on Saturday night because on Sunday everyone would be in church from nine forty-five until three o'clock singing praises to God.

While Mama and Cousin Ruth prepared today's dinner, I waited eagerly for Daddy. He always gives me a surprise before sitting down to his usual routine of polishing everyone's shoes for church. How Daddy can shine shoes! He shines everyone's shoes and sets them on the hearth. The glow from the flames give the shoes a magical luster.

Only this Saturday night Daddy didn't come home at his usual time. Mama continued cooking, but occasionally, while twisting her apron in apprehension, she would peer out the window.

After making countless trips to the window, Mama said, "I wonder where that man is. He knows we have to get ready for church."

Showing concern, Cousin Ruth said, "I hope nothing's wrong with George."

Mama immediately snapped, "Oh, I'm sure nothing has happened to him. He's probably somewhere having a good time."

"Maybe not, Candy. This isn't like George."

"I just know he better come home soon, or he'll be going to church by himself tomorrow. I'm tired. It's midnight and I'm not waiting another minute."

"I'm worn out, too," Cousin Ruth said. "Off to bed everyone," ordered Cousin Ruth.

We reluctantly went to our rooms. My three brothers share the back bedroom. I sleep with Cousin Ruth. I love sleeping with her except when I have nightmares. She makes me get out of bed immediately and read the twenty-third Psalms.

Last night I didn't want to go to bed because I knew Cousin

Ruth would have to make me read the Bible. I imagined all kinds of misfortunes had befallen my Daddy. He had been shot. No, he had been the victim of a hit and run driver. The horrible scenes were unceasing. I closed my eyes and pulled the cover over my head, but nothing could blot out the sinister pictures in my mind. Finally, sleep overwhelmed me and I drifted off momentarily. Then I heard it—an awful noise. Someone was trying to sing:

> "I'm slipping in—
> Please don't make that noise
> I'm slipping in—
> I been balling with the boys
> My mama, my mama
> Boy, she'll understand
> But my wife
> Will raise all kinds of sand."

As I sat up in bed puzzled, I heard Mama say disgustedly, "That's George. He's been drinking again." I tiptoed to my door, eased it opened, and listened. As usual, I was not disappointed. Mama turned off the living room light and stood three feet from the door waiting for Daddy. He slowly turned the key in the lock and tiptoed into the room. Just as he thought he had sneaked in, Mama turned on the light.

"George, where have you been?" She shouted. "Do you know what time it is?"

Sweat popped out on Daddy's forehead, but he didn't say anything.

"Here I am trying to get dinner ready for tomorrow," Mama continued. "And you're out prowling around only God knows where!"

Cousin Ruth woke up and started singing. She always sings the same song whenever something goes wrong:

> "Oh do not let
> This world depart
> And close thine eyes
> Against the light.
> O sinner, harden
> Not your heart
> Be saved tonight.
> Oh why not tonight?
> Oh why not tonight?
> O, sinner harden
> Not your hear, and
> Be saved oh tonight."

"Where have you been all this time?" Mama demanded.

"I would have been home hours ago, but I met an old friend of yours," Daddy mumbled.

"Who?" Mama asked.

"Miss Lucy," Daddy answered. "She asked about you and the children. She wants to come visit you."

Daddy kept his charade up for several minutes as Mama's lips began to quiver.

"I'm so glad you told me that," she finally said, sounding relieved.

Daddy added, "I told her you'd be happy to hear from her."

"No wonder it took you so damn long to get home," Mama snapped.

"What do you mean?" Daddy questioned.

"I mean Miss Lucy is in Heaven or Hell. She died three months ago!"

Before Daddy could say anything, Mama was all over him, beating him and growling like a grizzly bear. Daddy stumbled backwards and struck his head on the coffee table. Mama left the room crying. I wanted to go to Daddy, but I didn't want Mama to think I was taking sides. I just wanted to be sure Daddy wasn't dead. I didn't sleep well last night. I worried about him all night long. When I got up this morning Mama and Daddy were sitting at the kitchen table drinking coffee and sharing the newspaper. They were acting as if nothing had happened, and I was still upset. I will never understand grownups.

***

There's a new craze sweeping the country. It's called "The Twist." A stout guy named Chubby Checker created the dance. I suspect he was twisting his waist trying to lose weight while listening to the radio. Someone must have come by and seen him. "Show me how to do that!" must have been the request. Thus, a new dance was born.

Chubby Checker was on "The Ed Sullivan Show" last night dancing the twist. It looked like so much fun that I decided to try it. After the show I went to my bedroom and practiced in front of the mirror. I was proud of the way I looked as I sang the popular song.

"Come on, baby, lets do the twist. Come on, baby, lets do the twist. Take my hand and go like this."

Just as I began to sing the "round and round and round" part of the song, I saw a reflection in the mirror. I recognized my daddy. He had been standing in the dining room watching me all the time! He had an amused look on his face that embarrassed me. From now on I'll practice "the twist" behind closed doors. No matter what I have to do, I'm going to learn to do the twist.

*****

Fifth period was a total disaster today. I have completed eleven years of school without ever being sent to the principal's office, but today I almost spoiled my record. It wasn't really my fault. Shirlie made me angry, and I lost my temper. I can't tell Mama and Daddy because they would punish me. Mama says we are always responsible for our actions, so no excuse would be good enough for her.

I wonder how she would feel if her best friend was trying to steal her boyfriend? That is what Shirlie is trying to do. When Miss Simpson started class, Alice wrote me a note telling me that David walked Shirlie home yesterday. According to Alice, when Shirlie saw Alice walking behind them she began pushing David away and shouting for him to stop bothering her. I had planned to ask Shirlie to tell me her side of the story after class, but I never got the chance. When Shirlie saw us passing notes, she let her elbow hit my head.

"Excuse me," she said, loud enough for everyone to hear. Then under her breath she mumbled, "Miss Bookworm."

I didn't say anything because my parents taught me to ignore ignorance, especially when it deserves to begin with a capital "I". However, Shirlie seemed determined to infuriate me. She got up from her desk again. This time she needed to sharpen her pencil. As she passed by me on the way to her seat, she purposely dropped it on the floor. When she bent over to pick it up, she whispered, "David told me you're frigid."

I bent down so Miss Simpson could not hear what I said and whispered, "Kiss my ass."

She was dumbfounded. I never used that type of language, but I was tired of her and I wanted her to know it.

"What did you say?" She gasped.

I enunciated each word distinctly because I wanted her to get the full impact of what I had to say. I repeated my invitation to her slowly and deliberately.

I repeated, "I said kiss my ass."

She jumped up screaming, "Miss Simpson, you heard her. You heard her."

Miss Simpson turned around from the board and asked, "Shirlie, what are you talking about?"

"You heard her, Miss Simpson." She pointed at me. "She told me to kiss her ass."

"Hush your lying," Miss Simpson said. "I'm too tired on a Friday afternoon to entertain your nonsense."

Shirlie lost control. "I'm not lying. Everybody heard her."

No one said a word.

"Go sit down," Miss Simpson commanded.

She moped to her seat, but when she sat down she continued to mouth at Miss Simpson.

"You think she's perfect, but I know what she said." Then she looked Miss Simpson straight in the eyes and yelled, "You make me sick!"

Miss Simpson's next action surprised us. She hit Shirlie on the head with a textbook. Shirlie left the room crying and shouting back threats about what her mama was going to do to Miss Simpson.

On the way to our sixth period class, Alice asked me if I had actually said what Shirlie had accused me of. I denied it. I had no more time to waste on Shirlie *or* David. Chemistry would get my full attention, as it was one of the few courses I had to study.

Today wasn't a total loss. I learned to have faith in Mama's teaching. Mama says you should never let anyone know you completely. Everyone should know that I know all the words they know; I don't live in a vacuum. I just choose not to be a run-of-the-mill person. That's what Daddy calls people whose lives are as predictable as day follows night. Now, if getting into arguments had been a common practice of mine, Miss Simpson would have believed Shirlie. Because I had never been in trouble before, she didn't believe I was capable of acting disrespectfully. I got away with it this time. I must be careful not to have any more arguments with anyone.

After all, Mama always says "where there's smoke there's fire."

***

Rumors are rampant about Mr. Hart, our physics teacher. I guess we students are all to blame, especially me. Several weeks ago, Mr. Hart was told to take his class to the auditorium. When we got there, desks were scattered all over the gymnasium floor. Everyone was told to take a seat. No one said a word because we were all wondering why we were there. Several men came around and placed a booklet facedown on each student's desk. To my surprise, one of the men placed a test on Mr. Hart's desk. The spokesman for the group explained that we were going to take a physics test and that we should do our very best. Since physics is a required course I became very nervous; nevertheless, I tackled each problem with determination. At the end of the period, we were told to report to our next period class.

Although I had been busy working problems, I had kept glancing at Mr. Hart. He had started to work the problems but threw his pencil down with a gesture that suggested he had said "To hell with this!" Of course, the wrong message got out. Everyone is saying that he flunked the test and I made the highest score. I don't know what I made, and I really don't care. I applaud Mr. Hart for not taking the test. His rights were violated.

We've never heard any complaints about him. Physics is hard but all you have to do is study. He explains the material and gives us assignments to study at home. I really don't think the test had anything to do with his teaching. I'm the president of the student council, and I know he's had quite a few run-ins with the principal about students' rights. He's only asked for little things like more activities for students and permission to have representatives from the student council present at faculty meetings.

I think that's hardly reason to target him professionally!

***

Today's student council meeting was different. Mr. Hart didn't have much to say. The most exciting discussion we had was about painting the outside dumpsters black and orange and decorating them with a panther's face. Yes, all the meat has been taken out of our organization.

Some of the members are threatening to quit the council. I won't because I understand Mr. Hart's position. The principal has referred to him on several occasions as a trouble maker. Mr. Hart knows the principal thinks if he gets rid of him, he'll be rid of his problem. I would back off too. Mr. Hart has a wife and family to feed. He has to save money to send his children to college just like my parents do. Yes, it would be hard, but I would swallow my pride until the school term was over.

Then I would look for another job.

***

David comes around once in a while. Although we had a

misunderstanding I still miss him. That just proves you can get used to anything. David says I'm the only one keeping us apart. He says when I decide to act right, we can be special to each other again. By that he means for me to go all the way with him. To do that would be to violate every principle I've ever lived by. I already feel like damaged goods. What more does he want from me?

Grandmama used to tell me that no man wants a crushed flower, even if he crushes it himself! I can't let David crush me, at least not any more than he already has. I recited a poem in the fourth grade that seems to have been written especially for me. At the time, I learned it just to recite in the chapel program but it will stay with me always, especially since David has tried to exploit me. I wonder whether he knows what the word exploit means. Well, I won't give in. I'd rather be by myself. There are too many things I enjoy doing, like learning new vocabulary words and reading. I will stay strong and not become vulnerable. It's like the poem says, "Whatever happens, I want to be self-respecting and conscience free."

David's name pops up in Mama and Daddy's conversations sometimes. They miss him. He truly won everybody's heart. I not only lost a boyfriend, but the family also lost a handyman. All the errands and odd jobs David used to do, my parents are now having to do for themselves. He had played different roles in all our lives, leaving each one of us to miss him for a different reason. We had let our guards down, and he had invaded our home. In his anger, he had made accusations against my mother, planting suspicions about her fidelity to Daddy.

Our lives will never be the same.

CHAPTER 10
THE SAME OLD SONG—1961

For once in my life I wanted to do something different on New Year's Eve, but this one started out just like the rest. As usual, we prepared New Year's Day dinner. Most of our neighbors cooked black-eyed peas for dinner, but Mama always cooked collard greens with hog's jowl. She said peas represent pennies and greens represent dollar bills. She always looks forward to a prosperous new year. To my disappointment Daddy and Mama took us to watch night meeting to pray the new year in. As customary, they took sandwiches for everyone to enjoy. Sister Bellamy brought the coffee. I took a reluctant heart.

The night started off the same way it had for as long as I can remember. Deacon Bellamy gave the opening prayer. It was the same one he prayed every Sunday. It must have taken him a lifetime to memorize that prayer because he has never strayed from his script. I suspected he must have been Heaven bound because there was not a thing I could think of that he hadn't asked God to bless or provide for him.

I mouthed the words to his prayer as he thanked God "for waking me up this morning, for being clothed in my right mind, for putting food on my table, and for putting clothes on my back." He even asked God to bless the prison bound. That part of his prayer always amused me because it was rumored that Deacon Bellamy had been known to help himself to a few dollars when the offering plate was passed around. Nevertheless, he continued to pray for sinners. When he finished praying for every creature God had ever created, Sister Jefferson took over.

Sister Jefferson has skin that shines like patent leather and teeth as white as ivory. Lord, how she can sing! Last night she was in her best form. When she rose to her feet, everybody knew they were in for a treat. She started clapping and singing:

> "Guide my feet, Lord
> While I run this race.
> Guide my feet, Lord
> While I run this race.
> And I don't want to
> Run this race in vain."

When she finished singing the first verse, she started testifying while the congregation clapped to the beat of the piano.

She said, "You know, some of us go places we shouldn't go. We go to bars, clubs, and strip joints. Some of us even go miles away to gamble in casinos, throwing away money that could be used to feed the hungry, house the homeless, and help the widows and fatherless children."

Some congregation members shouted, "Amen, Sister Jefferson! Tell it like it is!"

With just a little encouragement, Sister Jefferson asked God to guide her tongue, her hands, and even her eyes. I wondered what other parts of her body she was going to ask God to guide before she finished singing. When she sat down, Sister Brown prayed and the congregation began to sing:

"I know it was the blood
I know it was the blood
I know it was the blood for me.
One day when I was lost
He died upon the cross and I
Know it was the blood for me."

Daddy prayed. To tell the truth, he wasn't any better than Deacon Bellamy. He also prayed for everything under the sun. When Daddy finished praying, we sang the second verse:

"The blood came streaming down
The blood came streaming down
The blood came streaming down for me.
The blood came streaming down
The blood came streaming down
And I know it was the blood for me."

I like the song because the words are easy to remember, but the picture of Jesus suffering like that always breaks my heart..

One by one each member of the congregation prayed. When I realized all the adults had prayed and it wasn't twelve o'clock, I got nervous. Gabriel and I were the only teenagers in the church. Several little children were seated on the mourning bench. Since they were too young to pray, I knew Gabriel and I would be called upon to pray next. I didn't mind saying a prayer I had memorized, but it was another thing to just up and start praying on the spur of the moment or from the heart with conviction.

When we finished humming a verse of "A Charge to Keep I Have," Deacon Bellamy nodded to me to pray. I didn't move.

Mama whispered to me to just say the Lord's Prayer. I got on my knees and recited the Lord's Prayer. To my surprise the experience hadn't been so terrible.

The congregation sang "Let Jesus Fix It." Everyone was encouraged to glorify God by lifting up our voice. I sang as lively as I could:

> "Let Jesus fix it for you and me
> He knows just what to do
> When so ever you pray
> Let him have his way
> And Jesus will fix it for you."

When we finished singing the first stanza, Deacon Bellamy called on Gabriel to pray. Gabriel was sitting on the last row neat the door. He got on his knees, closed his eyes, and clasped his hands under his chin. I thought to myself, this is going to be good. We hummed softly "Let Jesus Fix It" as we waited for Gabriel to begin praying. Gabriel said nothing. We hummed another verse of "Let Jesus Fix It." Still Gabriel said nothing.

Mama whispered to me to go to Gabriel and tell him to say "Lord, forgive my sins—anything!"

When I got to where Gabriel had been kneeling, he was gone. I noticed the door was slightly ajar. Gabriel had crawled out of the church! Mama and Daddy wanted to kill him. I thought the whole incident had been funny. Funny or not, I was sure of one thing. Deacon Bellamy would never call on Gabriel to pray again!

***

One disappointment after another has plagued my senior year. The first one was in October when I was not selected Miss

Purple and Gold. I can't explain it, but I really wanted to be queen. I have maintained an A average, excellent conduct, and high moral standards. Alice nominated me and Shirlie. As soon as Shirlie was nominated I knew I had lost the election. Mr. Hart told the class I was the only person who exemplified all the qualities a queen should have. I could tell he meant it from his heart, but unfortunately, elections are popularity contests, and Shirlie is more popular than I am. She has constantly reminded me that she is still a Lena Horne look-alike, and everybody loves Lena Horne.

My second disappointment happened today. I tried out for the senior play. I auditioned for the mother's role. Of course, Shirlie got the part. She took David from me, was chosen queen, and now has the leading role in the senior play. When will this nightmare end? No matter what happens I will not surrender to defeat or despair. In the end I am going to be victorious because I am smarter than she is, and I'm not hard to look at either. My skin is dark, but Mama says all honest Afro-Americans should be dark. Yes, I like the way I look, but I wish I wasn't so flat-chested!

***

My senior year hasn't been a total disappointment. I represented the Heroines of Jericoh in the district oratorical contest and won first place. This entitled me to represent our organization on the state level. I was very proud of my accomplishment because Mama and I wrote my speech. I wrote on the topic "Youth Meets the Challenges of Realizing his own Potential in a World Promoting Human Freedom and Dignity."

The state convention was held in town, so I had moral support. Mama is not a member of the Heroines of Jericoh, but she is always present whenever I perform. That makes me always do my best. She sits as close as she can get to the front in the middle aisle. When I speak, I look at her. The pride reflected in her face motivates me to dig down deep within myself and give my performances everything I have. It's as though my fear has taken wings and flown to unknown places.

Mama said she has never seen me perform more magnificently. She said she wished I could have seen myself. She said I was truly eloquent. I'm glad the audience couldn't see behind the podium, because all the time I was speaking my knees were shaking. I didn't feel afraid and my voice didn't quiver, but I couldn't stop my knees from shaking. There were six contestants. I was contestant number six. Mama said she could feel the tension all around her as each chapter pulled for its representative. Each time a speaker would finish, Mama said the man sitting next to her would say, "Now *that's* the best."

Mama said she told him, "You haven't heard the best yet."

Finally, my turn came. I walked to the podium, paused and took a deep breath as I searched for Mama's face. Somehow she had managed to sit on the fourth row in the middle aisle. Everything was perfect. I delivered my speech the way we had practiced it in the dining room at home. The head of the table had been my make-believe podium. Each gesture, voice reflection, or pause came out the way it had in our practice sessions.

When I finished, Mama said she turned to the bragging man sitting next to her and said, "Now *that* was the best."

To her surprise she said he answered, "I hate to admit it, but she was the best. But, how did you know?"

Mama said she gave a triumphant grin and said, "That's my daughter."

Not only did the man agree with Mama but the judges did, also. I won first place for the state of Georgia. Along with the honor came a two hundred dollar scholarship to be used at the college of my choice and a clock radio to wake me up on time for class. Now I'm thoroughly confused. I don't know whether to go to college or to go to California.

***

Miss Simpson must be a fool if she thinks I'm one. In January I tried out for the school play and was turned down. Instead, I was put in charge of props. Miss Simpson assured me that I had a very important job, but it doesn't take a genius to figure out that there is a difference between being the star of the show and placing some stupid props around. Now today she asked me to perform the second and third acts. She said Shirlie would still do Act I because she already knows it. It's Acts II and III she can't seem to remember. If it is possible to laugh inside one's body, I did.

She really amused me. She thought she knew how to psyche me out. She told me how badly the senior class needed me to play the part. To sum it up, according to Miss Simpson, I would be doing a noble deed for my fellow classmates, the school, and our community. It was my opportunity to be an angel on earth. I could have been kind and interrupted her, but I let her make a complete fool of herself. When she finally finished making her appeal, I gave her my answer.

"Miss Simpson," I began. "I would be honored to play the part if I had acting ability, but since I don't, I wouldn't want to embarrass myself or the class."

"But," she protested. "You're the only one who can learn the part on such short notice. I'm positive you can play the part."

"What makes you so sure? I asked. Then the devilish side of me added," I haven't taken any acting lessons."

"Are you sassing me?"

"No, ma'am," I protested. "I'm simply speaking the gospel truth."

I couldn't wait to get home and tell Mama the whole story. To my surprise, Mama invited me to a cup of coffee. There was no warning me that coffee would make be black. Instead, we sat around the table and shared stories.

Mama has suffered many of the indignities that had plagued my school days. She said she could remember several teachers who had favorites. She said they usually picked their friends' children or students who could afford to dress better than others. Mama said she always looked nice, but most of her clothes were homemade. She especially remembered a home economics teacher that gave her a hard time.

Mama said she made her friend Evangeline and her sweep the halls every day with heavy push brooms. Mama said they obeyed her until an upper classman told them that sweeping halls was punishment for being tardy to school. The next day when Mrs. Galloma told them to sweep the halls, Mama said they refused. She told them to get out of her classroom and not to return. They went to the principal's office and explained what had happened. He took them back to the classroom. Before he left, he told Mrs. Galloway that he wanted to see her in his office before the day was over.

Mama said Mrs. Galloway never had them sweep the halls again, but she got even in other ways. The first thing she did was to take Mama's grade. She said she did all her projects on time but could never make above a C. Every grading period she would question her grade, and Mrs. Galloway would say she had made a calculation error. Mama said she would change the grade on her report card, but she was sure the grade was not changed in Mrs. Galloway's roll book.

She carried out her final act of revenge during the end of year celebration. Mama said she split a part with another student in the school play. After the play Mrs. Galloway gave certificates for drama. Of course, Mama didn't receive one. This became the trend of the evening. For one reason or another, Mama said she managed to give everyone in the class an award except her and her friend Evangeline. Mama said her only regret was that she had participated in the play.

Before we washed dishes, Mama made me promise not to take the part in the play. I promised I would say no until hell freezes over!

***

Within a couple weeks I'll be leaving for California. It will be a relief to get away from the anger in this house. Mama and Daddy had another disagreement last night. Usually Mama starts the arguments, but Daddy did it this time. The whole incident didn't make any sense to me. I guess he is still suspicious because of the gossip David had repeated about Mama.

Mama attends summer school at Fort Valley State College. She's trying to complete the requirements for a B.S. degree in elementary education. Summer school ended yesterday. Mama called Daddy and told him she would be home around six o'clock. Six o'clock came and went, but Mama didn't come home. Daddy began to pace the floor and sip his corn liquor. The longer he paced the more corn liquor he sipped. I kept praying for Mama to come home soon because I had a feeling something awful was going to happen.

Mama didn't get home until after ten o'clock. That is

when all hell broke loose. As soon as Mama reached the porch, Daddy was out the front door and in her face, asking her why she was so late. She tried to explain that it had been raining cats and dogs, and Mrs. Miller couldn't see two feet in front of her. Mrs. Miller had pulled off the highway in Perry and waited for the rain to let up.

Then Daddy asked the stupidest question I have every heard him ask in my life. He asked Mama why it had rained in Perry but not here in Valdosta. Now, anyone with an ounce of sense knows it doesn't rain all over the world at the same time. Why, I've been standing on our back porch and seen it raining in Miss Caroline's yard, and it was as dry as Texas sand in our yard. Mama must have thought Daddy's question was stupid, too, because a large vein popped out on her forehead. She threw her head back and screamed as loudly as she could. That is when Daddy slapped her. It was the first time Daddy had ever hit Mama. She stared at him in disbelief. She had always been the one to do the hitting. Despondent, she sank onto the swing and cried uncontrollably. Daddy retreated in shame. He had always preached to my brothers that a man should never hit a woman, no matter what she had said or done to him.

Cousin Ruth went out on the porch to comfort Mama. Mama gave a tearful account of what had happened before she had reached home. She said the entire night had been a nightmare. After the rain had let up, she, Mrs. Miller, Mrs. Bacon, and Mrs. Calhoun had started out for home talking about summer school. They were saying things like, "I'm glad summer school is over. I wonder what grade I'll make." They were still talking about summer school when they noticed a blue light flashing behind them. Mrs. Miller pulled to the side of the road.

When she rolled down her window, a police officer asked

to see her driver's license. Mrs. Miller started pleading her case against speeding, but the officer told her that he had not stopped her for speeding. He said she had made a left turn without giving a signal. Mrs. Miller explained that her left signal was not working, but she had given a hand signal. The officer told her she knew her arm was too black for anybody to see at night, so she should tie a white handkerchief around it next time. Mama said they laughed with the officer at his racial joke, and he had sent them on their way without giving Mrs. Miller a ticket. I didn't know a natural occurrence like rain could cause such disturbance in people's lives. In a way, I should have known from Daddy's sermons about Noah and the Ark. I wonder what he'll preach about tomorrow. Repentance? Hypocrisy?

CHAPTER 11—THE BEGINNING—1995

"For you shall go out in joy, and be led forth in peace;
the mountains and the hills before you shall break forth into
singing.
and all the trees of the field shall clasp their hands."

Isaiah 55:12

I did not go to California. I went much further. How does
one measure the distance of a journey of self-exploration
and discovery? My experiences while living in South
Georgia helped me to develop a sense of self that would enable
me to travel anywhere in the universe and feel at home. My
background of turmoil, confusion, and poverty, deeply rooted
in love, gave me the thick skin that made me able to ward
off ignorance, prejudice, injustice, and double standards as I
pursued my goals.

There is no place on earth that I could visit that could ever
compensate for what I have accomplished. In 1966 I received
a B.S. degree from Fort Valley State College in Fort Valley,
Georgia. In 1978 I received the Masters of Education from
West Georgia College in Carrollton, Georgia. I later studied at
other colleges and universities. A sense of profound satisfaction
filled my heart because I knew that was just the harbinger of
joys yet to be.

I was ecstatic. I marveled at the barriers I had overcome

in my struggle for equality in a white-controlled society. I felt like an African queen with the world as my throne. I was the embodiment of Rosa Parks, Althea Gibson, Fannie Lou Hamer, Harriet Tubman, Sojourner Truth, and Mary McCleod Bethune, taking the barest threads of opportunity and turning them into advantages.

I was also proud that I had been born at a time when there were defined male and female roles. My brothers had been responsible for cutting the grass, raking leaves, and doing other outside chores. In contrast, ironing, washing, mopping, making beds, and completing indoor tasks had been my responsibilities. As man's role in society changed, I watched my brothers learn to cook, iron, and perform tasks previously referred to as "women's jobs". Having been a part of both cultures helped me to balance my role in life. This new attitude freed me to learn to be an assertive, strong-willed, self-sufficient individual, while at the same time, allowing me to maintain my femininity.

Gone is my concept of beauty—a blue-eyed blonde strolling along a beach in California during the day and returning to a hillside villa at night. I now flaunt my ebony skin, marvel at my broad nose, and revere my voluptuous lips, features that broadcast my strength and regality. They announce that historically I have journeyed from survival to glory with sweat and tears.

I am ever thankful for my new awareness, but the bittersweet years are intertwined in my soul, sometimes raging to be free. It is those bittersweet years that continue to sustain my zest for life. Whenever I am tired, disgusted, or depressed, I am able to draw from my anger and to remind myself that no matter how dark that day may appear I have faced darker days. Likewise, I am able to draw from the humorous events in my past life to remind me not to take myself or life too seriously. I am able to draw from the love I received from Grandmama, Mama, Daddy, Noah, Gabriel, Matthew, and all the other individuals who enriched my life to enable me to reach out to the homeless, a troubled child, the elderly, and victims of natural disasters, always mindful that I am truly blessed.

When in doubt, I am able to draw from the countless sermons I heard my daddy preach. The scripture that has influenced my beliefs the most is found in Jeremiah 29:11:

"For I know the plans I have for you, declares the Lord, plans to
Prosper you and not to harm you, plans to give you hope and a future."

Through my experiences, I know that God always keeps his promises. He has great plans for me. My previous accomplishments have only been pebbles making ripples in a mighty stream. There is nothing beyond my grasp. I can climb higher and higher. The sky is the limit!